D1239012

HOW TO INVEST SOMEONE ELSE'S MONEY

Other Business One Irwin Books of Interest:

Investment Policy, 2nd Ed. *By Charles Ellis*
Managing Your Investment Manager
By Arthur Williams, III
Asset Allocation *By Roger Gibson*
The Business One Irwin Guide to The
Wall Street Journal *By Michael Lehmann*
The Complete Words of Wall Street *By Allan Pessin*
and Joseph Ross

HOW TO INVEST SOMEONE ELSE'S MONEY

John W. Guy, CFP

IRWIN
Professional Publishing
Burr Ridge, Illinois
New York, New York

Project editor:	Denise V. Santor
Assistant production manager:	Jon Christopher
Art coordinator:	Heather Burbridge
Compositor:	BookMasters, Inc.
Typeface:	11/13 Times Roman
Printer:	Book Press

Library of Congress Cataloging-in-Publication Data

Guy, John W.
   How to invest someone else's money / by
John W. Guy.
      p.   cm.
   Includes bibliographical references and index.
   ISBN 1-55623-952-1
    1. Trusts and trustees. 2. Investments. 3. Corporate governance.
I. Title.
HG4309.G89   1994
332.6—dc20   93–10843
                                            CIP

Printed in the United States of America
1 2 3 4 5 6 7 8 9 0   0 9 8 7 6 5 4 3

ACKNOWLEDGMENTS

There are so many:

Jim Cooner of the Bank of New York and money manager Roger Gibson, authors both, who inspired me by their work and offered valuable advice.

My Dean Witter associates Kathy Birk, Burt Fendelman, Robert Palleschi, and Donna Coomes, who read, supported, encouraged, and advised.

Paul Zoschke of Alliance Capital Management, Marjorie Meyer of Hanover College, Mark Talt of U.S. Trust, and John Carver of Carver Governance Design for generating positive ideas.

Janet Cranc and members of the board of the International Association for Financial Planning, who kept me informed and provided valuable learning experiences.

Chris Katterjohn, publisher of *The Indianapolis Business Journal,* for supporting my early writing.

Robert Payton and Robert Fogal of the Indiana University Center on Philanthropy, as well as Scott Evenbeck, Irv Levy, Harriet Rodenberg, and Mary Jane Brown, and Indiana University in Indianapolis, for facilitating a new adult education course for trustees.

Three individuals spent hours reviewing the manuscript: Lois Sherman, the Indiana University Center on Philanthropy; professional money manager and student of modern portfolio theory, Robert Dorris, Wallington Asset Management; and Jack Miller, J. P. Morgan Investment Management, Inc.

Each organization recognized in a footnote provided data and support available nowhere else. I sincerely thank all of them.

By placing personal confidence in me, my clients contributed to this book. They have my deepest gratitude.

Of course, my family, including Laura and Alexander who asked, "Dad, are you really writing a book?"; Cindy and Andre Fall, who offered tangible labor; Chico and Gabriella, who hugged me at the right moments; and Chichi, who never doubted it could be done.

John W. Guy

TABLE OF CONTENTS

INTRODUCTION

Can trustees improve rates of return? I think so. I believe trustees can realize superior investment results in five steps:

1. Understanding themselves as individuals and as investors.
2. Studying and improving organizational governance.
3. Acquiring a risk sense and accepting at least one theoretical approach to risk management.
4. Affiliating with investment experts and listening to their ideas.
5. Creating forums and disciplines for continuing education.

These suggested steps arise from a personal fascination with how things get done. The fascination probably started while I was studying political science and working for a U.S. senator in Washington. I found that Congress does get things done and that this giant committee has developed rules and traditions that facilitate accomplishment despite enormous personal and philosophical differences among its members.

My informal study of effectiveness continued during Peace Corps service in Santa Cruz, Bolivia, where I was an outsider trying to understand an unfamiliar society, to produce objective improvements through local institutions. I learned that Bolivians are just like us. Some are effective and others are not, but all respect volunteer action taken to meet community needs.

The transition from Peace Corps volunteer to investment professional was surprisingly easy because both activities require discovery of individuals and groups that will be successful. Just as an effective Peace Corps volunteer must know who has both the power and talent to make change, an investment professional must identify companies that will earn above-average profits. He or she must predict which companies can reach their goals, a task requiring a philosophy of management effectiveness.

My professional experience in selling securities to individuals and institutions also has made me wonder about effectiveness and achievement. Why does Investor A do better than Investor B? Why does one mutual fund or private money manager excel? This book provides answers, especially for trustees. It suggests specific methods to make investment committees more efficient and effective. It proposes that boards and investment committees examine themselves at least as thoroughly as they study investment markets because inefficiently governed committees cannot achieve superior returns. Committees should merge theories of investment policy creation with new ideas about organizational governance. These two disciplines are reaching maturity and should get married.

The 1990 Nobel Prize in Economic Sciences to Messrs. Markowitz, Sharpe, and Miller proclaimed that investment economics has come of age. In a series of papers starting in 1952, these men described definite relationships between risk and reward. They proved that diversification reduces risk. They created the language of investment policies by applying mathematical tools such as standard deviation and beta to measurement of investment risk. Known generally as modern portfolio theory, this work created words and concepts that are tools of both understanding and communication. Trustees use these tools to write their intuitive ideas about risk and investment goals with confidence that competent third parties will understand their intent.

Thanks to writers and consultants, most investment committees have investment policies. Law and regulation require written policies for employee benefit plans, and many nonprofits also have them. Inevitably, the policies prescribe asset allocation in language emanating from work by these Nobel laureates.

Meanwhile, authors and consultants have studied effective and ineffective boards. Books describe methods to improve board/committee productivity, usually by managing ends instead of means. There also is important literature about leadership, personal motivation, self-improvement, goal setting, board/staff relationships, and the role of directors and officers, as well as efficient communication and time management techniques. I include all these ideas under *governance*. I believe they are practical ideas.

Is it not self-evident that investment committees operating within an efficient system of organizational governance are more likely to utilize modern investment theories to achieve superior rates of return? Isn't it at least imaginable that a marriage between investment economics and governance theory will produce fine children?

CHAPTER 1

THE JOY OF SERVING AS A TRUSTEE OF INVESTMENTS

This is the true joy in life, the being used for a purpose recognized by yourself as a mighty one; the being thoroughly worn out before you are thrown on the scrap heap; the being a force of nature instead of a feverish selfish little clod of ailments and grievances complaining that the world will not devote itself to making you happy.

George Bernard Shaw

Being trusted is a joy. Exercising trust is also a joy. If someone asks, "Would you like to join the investment committee of _____?" by all means say yes.

Then start a diary. Write down the value of the investment account on the day you are appointed. You will note the value again at the close of each year. The differences will result from your time and talents.

Tens of thousands of people become trustees every year. Employee benefit plans, foundations, endowments, fraternal organizations, colleges and universities, museums, historical societies, religious organizations, private foundations, and nonprofit organizations such as trade associations all have assets requiring supervision. The amounts of such assets vary from less than $10,000 to over $1 billion.

Most trustees are volunteers. Even large companies have investment committees of volunteers from various departments; they are considered volunteers because investing is not their full-time job, but they meet periodically to give advice to the professional investment staff and to create policy.

For nonprofits, trustees are generous, loyal volunteers who believe in a cause and in the obligation to serve the community. They give their time because the work is useful, enjoyable, and challenging, and the benefits are both personal and intellectual.

Trustees of investments encounter the same personal benefits as volunteers for any other cause: new friendships and a wider view of life. The intellectual benefits, however, exceed those of any other volunteer activity because good investors are careful, logical thinkers. Imagine the challenges faced by a new trustee. To be effective, a trustee must:

- Learn the language of investing.
- Develop personal opinions and strategies useful to the committee and the board.
- Find a comfortable niche—a job or role that is both personally satisfying and productive for the committee.
- Act diplomatically both to conform to existing governance and to propose improvements.
- Grasp the essence of risk.
- Relate risk to reward by learning a theory of portfolio management and applying it consistently in good times and bad.
- Write clear, practical goals and policies.

These tasks are difficult, but inherent in their difficulty is an opportunity for personal improvement; the trustee gets a chance to learn about the economy, specific industries and businesses, the mathematical view of portfolio management and spending policies, and the long-range effect of today's investment decisions. This volunteer service also helps individuals to manage their personal portfolios and to acquire realistic attitudes that reduce unnecessary worry and doubt.

Participating in American life and helping direct its financial capital are examples of "being used for a purpose recognized by yourself as a mighty one." Serving as a trustee is at once both trying and exciting, frustrating and rewarding, exhausting and exhilarating. Therefore, if you are asked to serve, say yes. If you are not invited, request the opportunity. It can be one of the finest experiences of your life.

CHAPTER 2

ON THE NATURE AND
IMPORTANCE OF TRUST

Trust: Confident expectation of something, hope; a person on whom or thing on which one relies; to permit to remain or go somewhere or to do something without fear of consequences.

Trustee: A person, usually one of a body of persons, appointed to administer the affairs of a company, institution, etc.

The Random House Dictionary of the English Language, unabridged, 2nd ed.

Trust and *investment* are inextricably linked. Acceptance of the link is required to create a potentially successful investment program. Failure to trust, "to do something without fear of consequences," prohibits the assumption of normal human risk, limits investment potential, creates strain between individuals, and reduces the effectiveness of institutions.

The language of trust seems decidedly simple and innocent. It applies to basic relationships and appears in such statements as these: "I trust you"; "I believe that history is a reliable guide to the future"; "The business affairs of this organization can be reliably administered by the board of trustees"; or "I am confident that you and I can live together, make reasonable choices, and be happy 'until death do us part.' "

Despite their appearance of simplicity, straightforward declarations of trust are difficult to apply to the world of investment risk. That special, unique world is divided into at least three nations. The first is populated by those who refuse to take any chances at all; the second, by those who believe they can predict the future by referring to charts, graphs, economic theories, and historical "waves"; and the third, by individuals who measure risk and then carefully allocate assets according to their risk tolerance. Citizens of these three nations speak different languages, seldom communicate, and occasionally either engage in wars of words or acquiesce silently. Since they *feel* differently, they respond differently and find it difficult to trust.

Meanwhile, the investment world trades mysterious assets. These assets are called *intangibles* because they are not themselves real. Stocks, bonds, and their derivatives provide only a financial participation in reality, and it is difficult to trust these instruments without a solid comprehension of their relationships to real economic activities. It is like the movie cowboy said: "If I can't feel it, smell it, or see it, I don't trust it." Similarly, many individuals say, "I don't understand the market. I don't trust it." They place personal funds in banks, collectibles, precious metals, or real estate. They have confidence only in assets that are real.

Investment committees and their advisors meet in this odd world of competing nations that trade mysterious assets. Trustees come to the table with different beliefs and different *feelings* and with a goal to create theoretical structures around intangible objects. Designing a strategy to invest is not like designing a car, selling a home, marketing a product, or establishing a new business. Instead, investment committees deliberate about the intangible and the theoretical. The experience is not always satisfying.

This is why routine meetings between investment committees and money managers often degenerate into one-way lectures about sophisticated economic models, strategies for selecting stocks and bonds, and past performance. They feature detailed questions and answers about one or two specific investment decisions that, in aggregate, barely affect total results. Occasionally, trustees directly show mistrust by firing a money manager who has not done well recently and hiring one whose recent results are better. Participants may also depart wondering if their time was well spent or feeling resentful that no one listened to their point of view or attempted to explain why things are as things are. The victim in each case is our old friend *trust,* the one who makes investment possible.

Because they have no choice but to trust someone or something, trustees should raise trust to its well-deserved position of honor and respect. Assuming responsibility for money inherently and absolutely implies a need to trust a host of people and principles, including:

Our way of life.
The nature of economic growth.
The advantages of diversification.
Our fellow decision makers.
Historic data.
Ourselves.

Without confidence in these and other standards, we as trustees must either give up any attempt to improve our lives through positive invest-

Wealth Indices of Investments in the U.S. Capital Markets (1925–1992)

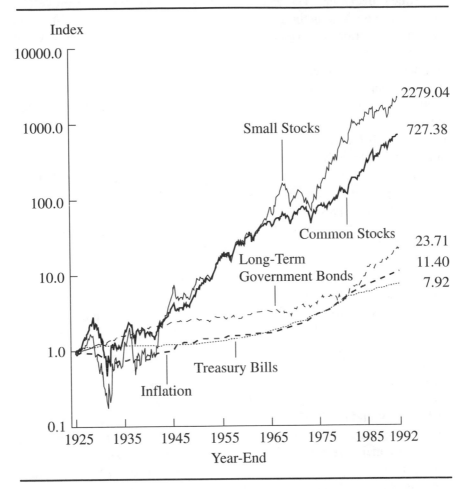

Source: Ibbotson Associates

Wealth measurements from 1925 to 1992 provide a basis for trust in securities markets. Of course, the best returns were earned from the most volatile assets. This graph uses a logarithmic scale on the vertical axis that compresses recent results. On a linear scale, the ending values of small stocks and common stocks would appear several feet above the top of this page.

ments or abdicate decision-making responsibilities to others who are able to get the job done, precisely because *they* have in fact decided where to place their trust.

First, we must trust our way of life. We must believe that our institutions will survive and will constantly provide a logical framework for investment decisions. These institutions are a medium for transactions (stock exchange), a method of transferring value (money), a predictable system of taxation, the means of communication such as telephones and computers, and a relatively stable government. There also must be confidence in economic growth at its most fundamental, a faith that the increasing population will naturally produce more goods and services while technology fosters increases in per capita production. We must believe that each of us will accomplish more per hour in the future than we can accomplish today or, at least, that some of us—the ones to whom we should delegate both our trust and our capital—will be more productive.

However, for safety and peace of mind, we also must trust that not everything we try to do will work out. This may seem a perverse sort of trust, but it is a reality that merits continuous attention. Although we must believe in economic growth, it also is certain that some efforts will fail and that some products and services useful and popular today will not be around tomorrow. We know this. We trust in this. Therefore, we prudently apply a standard of diversification so that our lives and fortunes never depend on a single activity.

We also must trust our fellow decision makers, including our spouses, children, colleagues, and those with whom we serve as directors and trustees. This is particularly challenging when investment capital is at stake, as demonstrated by widows and widowers who have no personal experience in family finance because they delegated money matters to their spouses. Boards do it, too. They delegate investment policy creation and implementation to a minority who, by job or reputation, appear qualified or at least seem to understand the language of professional investing. Often, creating and implementing investment policy are the only management functions totally delegated to a committee. The entire board retains responsibility for other tasks, such as fundraising and budgeting, because all board members are comfortable discussing basic administration, but few understand investing. The majority delegates absolute control over investment policies. The majority says, "Investment committee, we trust you (since we don't trust ourselves)!"

Trust in data also is important. Historic data is the only reference point for designing personal or institutional investment programs, yet many people have no confidence in securities markets statistics. They might trust recent information, but not long-term statistics. The problem is memory.

Idealists compare securities markets to weather, because everyone has faith in weather fundamentals. There is universal acknowledgment that summer is warmer than winter, that some summers are warmer and wetter than others, and that disastrous droughts or floods happen every once in a while. On the other hand, millions of people do not accept comparable phenomena in the securities markets. Even though the long-term data implies orderly growth, logical relationships (especially price compared to earnings), and the inevitability of abnormal occurrences, there is a powerful human tendency to make decisions based only on yesterday's events. Therefore, every change is a surprise. Every deviation from a recent trend prompts apprehension or fear. Imagine the fear of an individual who remembers only yesterday's thunderstorm or tornado and forgets the long-term consistency of seasonal weather changes. Imagine the position of an investor who recalls only aberrations such as the decline of 1973–74 or the crash of 1987. It is impossible to build trust from such limited data.

Trustees build investment strategies based on both historic data and confidence in the optimistic message of that data, which is that securities markets are cyclical, have fluctuated around broad norms of performance, and are likely to continue doing so. Trustees must acquire this confidence. It is an obligation. Effective investing is impossible without it.

The accumulation of trust in external realities inexorably leads to trust in oneself and in one's own ability to design an investment program that fits personal or institutional circumstances and responsibilities. This is why trust and investments are linked. One would not acquire an investment asset if one did not trust that there would be a profitable conclusion. Trustees cannot purchase securities for themselves or for others without confidence in both their ability to understand markets and the probability of long-term success.

Fortunately, those who do become active in formulating investment policies rapidly build confidence in both people and principles, and they soon find personal satisfaction, larger profits, and trust in themselves.

CHAPTER 3

DO TRUSTEES ADD VALUE?

The cause is hidden, but the result is well known.

Ovid

It is disquieting to propose that money managers and boards of trustees subtract value. Nevertheless, it may be true. Some authors have mentioned the problem. In 1985, distinguished consultant Charles Ellis observed that "disagreeable data are steadily streaming out of the computers of the performance measurement firms. . . . The nation's investment managers are not beating the market; the market is beating them."[1] In 1992, the Brookings Institution affirmed Ellis's hypothesis by stating that "the picture of the pension fund industry that our analysis has painted is not a positive one. As far as performance is concerned, pension fund equity managers seem to subtract rather than add value relative to the performance of the S&P 500 Index."[2]

These experts have stated in print a notion that has appeared for years in backroom conversations among professional investors. The notion is that professionally managed investment accounts do not perform as well as the averages. In other words, it is possible to earn fine returns by purchasing securities and holding them forever without continuous, expensive supervision. Stated another way, it is impossible to "beat the market" because transaction costs and normal human errors reduce returns that would have been achieved by leaving things alone.

Blame for below-average performance has been placed on professional money managers, but money managers are merely the quarterbacks on teams that include boards, investment committees, consultants, and staffs. Each of these team members sometimes acts on unsolicited advice from company owners, plan beneficiaries, and outside observers such as social action groups. Therefore, how do we know who subtracts value? Let's review the possible culprits.

CONSULTANTS

Professional consultants are among the brightest individuals in the investment business, and they have contributed significantly to both the theory and practice of investing. They have appropriately encouraged the creation of written investment and spending policies, and they have invested millions of dollars to provide computer power for both performance measurement and analysis of theory. Most consultants have useful opinions about effectiveness because their clientele includes both weak and strong plan sponsors. They can see and describe the differences. If consultants subtract value, it would be because:

1. Their fees are too high compared to the services they render.
2. They promote needless services; for example, they encourage clients to replace investment managers or to add new managers unneccessarily.
3. They provide more data than needed.
4. They are afraid to say what they really think out of fear of losing a client.

PROFESSIONAL MONEY MANAGERS

Money managers are the front line. They are extremely well-educated, dedicated soldiers who work extra hours both to discover profitable investments and to satisfy clients' personal and administrative requirements. However, they are vulnerable. Their clients can be notoriously disloyal, dismissing them for a single down year out of many good ones. If professional money managers subtract value, it would be because:

1. It is not feasible to beat an average consistently, because each manager's results are part of the average.
2. Overcoming the negative effect of transaction costs and fees is too large a hurdle.
3. Managers invariably hold cash positions, often in the 2 percent to 10 percent range. In a rising market, uninvested cash reduces performance compared to an index.

4. There is no practical method to predict with certainty who will be superior. We know outstanding money managers, the Mozarts of investing, only by hindsight.

PLAN SPONSOR'S INVESTMENT STAFF

Because there is no consistency of function between institutions, it is not possible to evaluate staff. While financial staffs of educational institutions appear to have little influence over endowment investment policy, the treasury staffs of large companies appear to make many important decisions. Meanwhile, there is literature criticizing staffs, most rendered by outside observers, but insiders seldom provide written points of view.

Critical comments include these from Brookings:

> The corporate insiders who allocate the money must worry about their own jobs and reputations. The performance of the assets in the pension plan will influence their future success with the company. . . . The treasurer's office has a bias against [inexpensive] passive management because passive management reduces the demand for services produced by that office and thus reduces the size of its empire. . . . The treasurer's office [also] has a bias against internal management of money and for delegation. External management may make good sense because it permits the realization of economies of scale and allows flexibility to switch between many money managers with various investment styles. In addition, the treasurer's office wants to delegate money management in order to reduce its responsibility for potentially poor performance of the plan's assets.[3]

These observations cannot be proved, but they do have intuitive legitimacy. The primary goal of all bureaucracies is to protect themselves. Nevertheless, whether staffs add or subtract value is unknown.[4]

TRUSTEES

There is no reliable, consistent, objective information about trustee involvement in investment decisions. However, it is very likely that trustees subtract value when their work is compared to results of passively managed accounts or mutual funds. If trustees do subtract value, it would be because:

1. Investment committees involve too many individuals who compromise with one another at the lowest common denominator. Often a committee's decision reflects a consensus that none of the participants would have supported independently.
2. Investment committees and individual trustees interfere with the ideal investment process by writing inappropriate policies, placing unnecessary restraints, and requesting excessive services and attention from their investment managers.
3. Trustees meet infrequently and communicate poorly with each other. Their decisions are unduly biased by beneficiaries who want only immediate financial support (a spending policy that distributes large amounts of cash each year) and have little sensitivity to long-term growth.
4. Trustees are unwilling to assume even average market risks for fear that potential losses would damage their personal credibility.

The judgment that trustees subtract value may be shocking, but it is also unfair and irrelevant, for the thesis of this chapter and this book is that trustees can add value (or subtract less value) by learning how to invest and how to govern themselves. Because they are players on a complex team, trustees should not assume all of the blame, if blame there be. On the other hand, trustees can improve their work, if only because all people or all committees can improve themselves. Simple, direct, unencumbered decision making is efficient governance, which is likely to produce superior investment results. The proof starts with the following list of investors, ranked from most efficient to least efficient.

1. *Individual investors* are free to buy what they want, when they want, with few consultations or policy restraints. They are the most efficient investors. Individuals who practice professional money management, either as independent executives with discretion or as managers of private partnerships, also are efficient, and some have achieved legendary success. Biographies have been written about individual investors, but not about investment committees.

2. *Mutual funds* are managed in private offices separated from their owners, who are "members of the public." Mutual fund managers have no direct contact with their owners (individual investors and plan sponsors) because either brokers or clerks handle all transactions and questions. Therefore, mutual fund managers make investment decisions in a physical and intellectual environment dedicated entirely to security selection. They are not affected by the personal circumstances of owners such as income needs and tax brackets. Unlike private money managers, who separately manage numerous accounts, mutual fund managers oversee only one account. They do not directly conform to variant investment policies of different owners. Instead, they abide by one set of investment policies normally described in a prospectus, and their only goal is to earn respectable total rates of return.

3. *Private money managers retained by employee benefit plans* are hired by trustees who usually work for the same company and communicate easily with one another. The opinions of other employees and company officers may influence these trustees, but most employees simply want positive rates of return and have minimal interest in policy. Money managers meet with trustees once or twice a year during business hours in a business setting. Many trustees speak the language of investing, which facilitates good communication. These private money managers have learned how to meet two challenges: to communicate well with clients and to meet or exceed actuarially prescribed investment goals.

4. *Private money managers retained by endowments and foundations* must deal more frequently with clients. Nonprofits demonstrate both a strong need to express investment policy (i.e., to place guidelines on money managers) and cumbersome governance. Trustees usually are volunteers who do not know each other well and meet infrequently. Occasionally it is unclear who is in charge or whether a specific decision may be made by a staff officer or by the board. Therefore, it sometimes takes a long time to arrive at a conclusion.

5. *Money managers working for public funds,* such as public employee retirement plans, must meet with boards that are heavily influenced by normal problems of governance as well as by local politics. Federal, state, and local laws and ordinances, as well as numerous executive orders and written policies, control all investment decisions.

The differences between these categories are not in past investment performance, intelligence, creativity, or competitive zeal. Instead, they are differences in the structure of human relationships. The most efficient investors are the least governed. The least efficient deal with both complicated written restrictions and the dynamics of boards and committees. Efficiency results from quick and easy decision making; minimum constraints on money managers; and limited contact between plan sponsors and money managers, because personal meetings waste time that could be better applied to analysis and portfolio management. Inefficiency oc-

TABLE 3–1
Annual Return of Equity Funds of Pension Plans and Percentage
Underperforming S&P 500, 1983–1989

Year	Equally Weighted Return Across Funds	S&P 500 Return	Funds Underperforming S&P 500
1983	17.8	22.5	59%
1984	3.8	6.3	63%
1985	33.3	32.2	38%
1986	18.1	18.5	50%
1987	4.0	5.2	61%
1988	17.9	16.8	47%
1989	29.2	31.5	61%
Mean	17.7	19.0	54%

Courtesy: The Brookings Institution.

The above figures overstate equity fund performance compared to the S&P 500 for two reasons. Most plans maintain cash in the equity account that reduces total returns. Also, management fees averaging 50 basis points (½ of 1 percent) on actively managed accounts and 25 basis points on index funds have not been deducted.

curs when owners interfere with investment decisions by imposing burdensome policies and requiring costly meetings and reports. Inefficient governance involves unproductive activities that directly reduce performance, incur unnecessary costs, or divert attention of investment professionals to reporting, marketing, and hand-holding.

Do results support these rankings? Yes, but not conclusively, because the data is sparse. There is no reliable data about investment returns earned by individuals investing their own funds, and information about institutional results comes from different sources using different methods of collection and interpretation.

Mutual funds appear to have done better than endowments.[5] According to Morningstar, 28 funds classified as balanced had an average annual return of 15.41 percent from July 1, 1982, through June 30, 1991. The composition of these funds ranged from 79 percent/27 percent to 15 percent/70 percent stocks and bonds, respectively.[6] Therefore, balanced mutual funds may be similar to endowments but with one important difference: Mutual funds usually reinvest dividends, but endowments and foundations withdraw income.

Brookings has reported pension fund data for the five-year period 1983–1989. The equity portion of pension funds returned 17.7 percent for the years 1983–1989, compared to 19 percent for the S&P 500.[7] This pension fund data is not comparable to the endowments or balanced mutual funds mentioned above because it reports only equities and measures a different period. However, it marginally supports the hypothesis that trustee-directed, actively managed accounts do not perform as well as indexes. The Brookings authors agree. They say,

> Our results on the inferior performance of pension fund equity managers are in complete accord with the historical evidence. In 1981 *Pensions and Investments* reported that 74 percent of the equity funds in the pension fund universe of Becker (SEI's predecessor) underperformed the *S&P 500* over the 1971–80 period. Gilbert Beebower and Gary Bergstrom report results for the 1966–75 period, although they do not seem to limit themselves to equity funds. They find that the average beta-adjusted performance of the pension funds lagged behind the *S&P 500* by approximately 150 basis points [1.5 percent] per year. Gary Brinson, L. Randolph Hood, and Beebower study the performance of 91 large pension plans over the 1974–83 subperiod. They find that performance of the funds lags behind the *S&P 500* by 110 basis points [1.1 percent] per year, with more substantial underperformance for the equity portion of the portfolios.

Then they compare results to mutual funds:

> The numbers reported by *Pensions and Investments* indicate that over the 1971–80 period (during which 74 percent of equity pension funds underperformed the *S&P 500*) only 42 percent of equity mutual funds did so. The mean annual return for the mutual funds over this period was 9.2 percent compared with 6.9 percent for the pension funds.

After presenting additional numbers, they conclude:

> These performance numbers for mutual funds look on the order of 50 to 100 basis points better than any of the numbers we reported for equity pension funds regardless of methodology or sample period. Taken together, this evidence leads us cautiously to conclude that mutual funds have outperformed pension funds, at least from the mid-1960s through the mid-1980s.

All this data, albeit inconsistent, hints at a possibility—no, a probability—that investors and investment firms perform best when left alone. Unmanaged indexes have done best, while independent, unfettered mutual fund managers have come in second. The reasons might be that returns decrease as governance becomes more complex and that money management is an art requiring independence and freedom. Theories of leadership make similar assertions. They say individuals perform best when told *what* to do, not *how* to do it.

Yet the data also creates doubts. It says that active money managers are not winning against indexes representing the entire stock market. The specific statistical comparisons suggest that owners and managers subtract value because their accounts do not perform as well as passive indexes. But are indexes the appropriate standard? Perhaps it would be better to compare performance to certificates of deposit or money funds. In this framework, committees and managers would earn high praise. There would be no question that trustees add value and provide an important administrative means for earning rewards by accepting risks.

Thus, we have a perplexity about the chapter title's question, Do trustees add value? In one sense they do, for the investment committee system is the accepted method of administering investment accounts. On the other hand, performance data suggests that trustees subtract value, that the more people involved in a decision, the weaker the results.

I believe that each board of directors or retirement plan advisory committee should specifically and directly resolve the perplexity by declaring in writing exactly what it wants to achieve:

- Does the board want to earn a stock market rate of return commensurate with market risk? If so, what is the least expensive method?
- Does it want to "beat the market" by assuming greater risk? Does it need higher rates of return to accomplish real-life goals such as superior educational or social services? If so, what is the best way to do it? Should the board have an investment committee, delegate authority to staff, or directly hire an investment coordinator or consultant to get the job done?
- Does the board need to avoid risk entirely? If so, it is easy and inexpensive for staff or a reputable investment company to buy short-term U.S. Treasury securities.

With clear directions, trustees soon will know if they add or subtract value; but to determine value, trustees also should calculate costs of their deliberations. They should determine the expenses of governance.

Imagine, for example, a proposed two-day investment committee meeting to interview 10 investment advisors. Potential costs are:

- Trustee transportation to the site.
- Trustee meals and lodging.
- Dollar value of trustee time.
- Cost of meeting space.
- Staff transportation, lodging, and meals.
- Advisor transportation, lodging, and meals ($\times$ 10).
- Value of advisor time ($\times$ 10).
- Cost of clerical support.

Estimating only moderate costs and value of time, the total financial burden of this meeting is staggering. In other words, inefficient governance itself subtracts value.

*   *   *   *   *

Trustees of investments wear foggy diving masks in a murky sea. Their masks are clouded by dozens of theories, preconceptions, and temperamental restraints. The sea is clouded by hundreds of statistics swimming in different directions, up and down, left or right, sometimes in circles, all telling different stories. Brokers, consultants, authors, money managers, and amateur investors seek attention, each suggesting the best direction to swim. But only the board of directors can indicate the correct direction. As a trustee of an organization, you add value when you state: "This is where we want to go. Take us there."

NOTES

1. Charles D. Ellis, *Investment Policy* (Homewood, Ill.: Business One Irwin, 1985), p. 5.
2. Josef Lakonishok, Andrei Shleifer, and Robert W. Vishny, "The Structure and Performance of the Money Management Industry," *Brookings Papers on Economic Activity* (Washington, D.C., 1992), p. 378.
3. Ibid., p. 342.
4. Criticisms of professional staffs are based on historic data, some quite old. The skills and expertise of staffs have been improving because retirement plan investment performance now affects reported corporate financial re-

sults, professional associations promote personal development through continuing education, and staffs now can apply modern portfolio theory.
Treasury staffs today are more experienced, and more young people are pursuing the investment profession.

5. This conclusion that one category of plan sponsor did better than another is
   only partially documented here. It is based on the author's perusal of both
   public and private data.

6. Data from Morningstar, Inc.; 53 W. Jackson Boulevard; Chicago, Illinois,
   60604. Phone: (800) 876-5005. The data does not include the negative effect
   on returns caused by front-end commission charges, but many funds do not
   charge front-end commissions on large purchases.

7. Lakonishok, "The Structure and Performance," p. 348.

8. Ibid., pp. 352–53.

CHAPTER 4

A MEETING OF THE "UNIVERSITY" INVESTMENT COMMITTEE*

When all was said and done, much was said, and little done.

Unknown

John Reimer and Doris Dock left New York in good spirits. It had been nine years since they first contracted to manage the endowment of the university, a 4,000-student school in the Midwest, managed by a 50-member board of trustees, a 26-member board of visitors, the faculty assembly of 350, and a staff committee including the president and the university controller, with occasional advice from the student congress, *The Daily Student,* and alumni upset over this or that.

John and Doris understood that this business opportunity was, at first, the result of both their respectable record of investment performance and a friendship between their boss and Joe Franklin, head of the university's investment committee and president of a large life insurance company, but they had done a good, consistent job that deserved respect and loyalty from the investment committee and the board of trustees. In short, they had a good story to tell, and it would be satisfying to explain their results, as well as their philosophies and projections for the next year or two. The committee would applaud their work. It was likely to be a very good day.

* * * * *

Joe Franklin was tired. Saturday afternoon committee meetings were getting to be too much, but in 1981 he had agreed to serve the university, to give it the benefit of his 35 years of experience in the life insurance business, and he wanted to keep that commitment. Public service was important to him. He was very active in his local United Way, chamber

---

*This is fictional.

of commerce, and Heart Association, and his company was a good corporate citizen, a source of support for many community activities. He personally was giving over 10 percent of his income to charities, and several years ago he privately told his wife that he enjoyed participating in community work more than managing the corporation.

Joe was optimistic that today's meeting would be short and to the point. He especially trusted First National Bank, the university's money manager. The bank's account representatives, John Reimer and Doris Dock, were smart and articulate, although they both seemed young for such a major responsibility. Unfortunately, he could not relieve his mind of problems at work, especially news from his investment director that three issues held in the bond portfolio were going to default. In addition, interest rates were falling, subjecting many of his high coupon bonds to early redemption. Therefore, those assets would be invested at lower rates, perhaps even below levels required to make a profit.

Things could be worse, he thought. At least I've kept the company out of junk bonds and have resisted pressures from the young guys to increase our involvement with common stocks. The stock market is too much for me. It makes no sense at all. Anyway, everything will work out just fine, and it is time to think about the university for a couple of hours.

*　*　*　*　*

University Controller Fred Brummett was apprehensive about today's investment committee meeting. He could not reconcile his own understanding of investment results with reports from the independent consultant and the money manager. His computation of appreciation, essentially a simple interest calculation, did not produce the same result as either the time-weighted or dollar-weighted methods employed by the consultant. Furthermore, he was uncertain whether the committee would compare results to the S&P index of 500 stocks, the more sophisticated Wilshire Index, or a popular average like the Dow Jones Industrials. He also was uncertain if the committee would count income as part of total return. But why worry? he thought. I'll just pass out my report and let the committee figure it out.

There's one thing, he thought. I wish the university had a policy precisely relating income and growth of the endowment to budgeted expenditures. Trustees on the budget committee frequently ask why we can't spend endowment principal on new buildings because real estate is a form of investment, and I'm often in the middle of the argument.

Personally, I sometimes feel that we spend too much, and other times too little. There should be a way to make sense of this.

*   *   *   *   *

Tom Balentine was prepared. A professional money manager himself, he felt it was clear that he had been appointed to the investment committee because of his special experiences. In his mind, he was one trustee who understood the investment business, its language, and the potential circumstances in which incompetence and fraud could create losses. In fact, he constantly looked for illegal or inappropriate sales tactics by registered representatives and financial planners, who, in his view, judged an investment only by the commissions it might generate for themselves. Almost every personal portfolio he reviewed revealed assets acquired through either misleading sales tactics or poor judgment. He saw the problem last Thursday in the portfolio of Georgia Schmidt, the widow of successful McDonald's restaurant owner Robert Schmidt, who had left her more than $2 million in securities. Over almost 40 years, Robert had saved regularly by purchasing stocks, bonds, and partnerships, including a few Tom viewed as outrageous scams. Though Robert had earned total annual returns in excess of 10 percent, Tom could not understand why Robert had acquired illiquid limited partnerships in oil and gas drilling, low-income housing, shopping centers, and wind power systems.

Robert should have purchased only quality stocks and AA-rated bonds, he thought. I'll never put anything so speculative in my clients' portfolios.

During the last two weeks, Tom had been reviewing reports about the university's endowment, transactions made in the last quarter, and return calculations provided by the consultant. He was certain he should make the investment committee aware of unfavorable comparisons between the endowment's total return and results of certain averages. He also wanted to call attention to three specific purchases that were not consistent with acceptable risk standards. Yes. He was ready for this meeting. He would have a lot to say.

*   *   *   *   *

Jim Nugent did not want his wife to leave today. There was a lot to do. The house was only half-painted, and the job should be completed this weekend. They should take the kids to the mall to purchase birthday gifts for their brother, while he personally needed time to prepare for next week's United Way meeting. But he did understand Mary's obligation.

Last year she had been appointed to the university's board of trustees and subsequently to the endowment investment committee. This made him proud. He knew that her tremendous loyalty to the university (as well as to its fraternal institutions), her willingness to make fund-raising calls on wealthy alums, and her head-of-the-class academic performance in finance and accounting prepared her well to become a conscientious steward of the university's assets.

Mary herself did not want to attend the meeting because, like Jim, she knew there were many other things to do, and the first meeting she attended last year was long and lacked direction or purpose. Nevertheless, the task itself—to invest capital wisely—was exciting and challenging. She looked forward to learning more about it. It definitely would be an interesting meeting for her.

* * * * *

JOE:

This meeting will come to order. Looks like everyone is here. Fred, Joe, Mary, as well as John and Doris, and the consultant. OK. Let's start. Fred has passed out financial reports, as well as the report from the consultant. Do you have any comments, Fred?

FRED:

Yes. I have reviewed data submitted by the money manager and the consultant, and have made calculations of rates of return. As you can see, Mr. Chairman, the three calculations produce different results. I believe the investment committee should direct that performance presentations be made in one manner by everyone giving us data, and that all data should be comparable to standardized indexes such as the S&P 500. Meanwhile, I continue to be concerned that we have no spending policy or other means to coordinate investment results with expenditures authorized by the budget committee.

JOE:

Thank you, Fred. Now, the first and most important agenda item is the presentation by our investment manager. John and Doris, the floor is yours.

JOHN:

Thank you, Mr. Chairman. We achieved the investment results shown in your packet during a time of great uncertainty, a period of transition in our economy, the nation, and the world. Interest rates were volatile, and currency changes made investing overseas especially difficult, but we were able to keep pace with our peers by strategically placing capital in . . . [10 minutes elapse] while avoiding pitfalls of the extreme movements witnessed in . . . [20 minutes], but our view is that the economy will . . . , interest rates will . . . , and inflation will . . . , and bond prices will . . . , and equities undoubtedly will . . . [30 minutes]. Now, Doris will comment on specific decisions, and I then will summarize.

DORIS:

Thank you, John. Last month, the beginning of the current quarter, we decided that conditions were becoming more favorable for investment in long-term bonds and small cap stocks, so we placed 35 percent of your assets in these categories, while maintaining previously established positions in . . . [40 minutes], but the investment environment did not improve as quickly as we had thought . . . [45 minutes]. Meanwhile, we reviewed our positions in pharmaceuticals, autos, and consumer cyclicals, selling selected issues in the belief that they had realized their full potential. Now, John will conclude [55 minutes].

JOHN:

Thank you, Doris. We are proud of our record this quarter because we were able to keep pace with our peers without increasing risk, and I will try to explain our total results briefly, within the one-hour time limit you have requested, but it is important to note that . . . , and we would like to tell you about our economic and market assumptions for the next quarter, but time seems to have run out, so we are ready to hear your comments and to answer any questions you may have. [Total elapsed time: 65 minutes.]

JOE:

That was an excellent report. Thank you for providing it, and for flying here today. In the interests of time, let's go directly to the report of the consultant, who is responsible for assisting us in determining asset allocation and evaluating money managers.

THE CONSULTANT:

Mr. Chairman, during the period, the endowment of the university performed slightly below the average for all endowments in its peer group, as shown on our handout. Our numbers include both funds handled by the manager as well as your permanent bond portfolio and cash. Results also were below popular market averages. For the 5- and 10-year periods, however, your results are in line with most other college and university investment accounts, but still below market averages.

You should be aware that several professors have been studying institutional investment activities, especially what they call "active portfolio management,'' and they believe there is a problem. They have been saying that active management does not produce results as good as passive management, often called indexing. Unfortunately, the subject is controversial, because no one has much more than 10 years of data, but I still recommend that you authorize us to study this further. We should calculate how your account would have done had it been indexed over the last 10 years. Then we should determine the risk and the volatility of the index, and compare this to the risk you assumed and the rewards you earned. I believe this would be useful.

There appear to be two reasons for your recent underperformance. The first is that you were not represented in the market sector commonly called small cap, which includes stocks of new companies in the first one third to one half of their growth curves. This sector did unusually well last year. The portion of other portfolios invested in this sector experienced total rates of return up to 60 percent, a phenomenal result that obviously pulled up the average for those accounts. Please note, however, that this sector had done poorly in each of the previous five years. Second, your manager decided to acquire securities of financial firms, such as banks and savings and loans, that did not do well, thereby lowering results compared to managers who avoided the financial sector.

TOM:

Why in the world did we acquire stocks of savings and loans, especially Home, Bank, and Lend? Everyone knew they were in trouble, and unlikely to do anything but go down. I did not permit my clients to buy them. Please, we must have an answer to this question.

DORIS:

Tom, we acquired these stocks because they were selling at the low end of their historic ranges, had low price-earnings ratios, and most were selling below book value. We simply felt that they represented good value, and we continue to feel that way today.

TOM:

So you have decided to risk our capital in an industry that has been involved with poor regulation, mismanagement, and possibly fraud, and that has been out of favor with the public for over five years? This does not make sense to me at all.

DORIS:

We frequently find value in out-of-favor stocks.

CONSULTANT:

Tom, your point is worthy of consideration, and we should focus on the future. We think—

JOE (interrupting):

Let's try to save our questions until the end. We also must consider the overall performance, not just specific transactions.

MARY:

This is an important point, Joe. I'm not sure whether my responsibility is to look only at the entire portfolio, or whether I should be concerned about specific stocks and bonds, but it would be very difficult for me to follow all these securities.

CONSULTANT:

Mary, generally we believe trustees should look at the total result, but they also should assure themselves that managers do not make investments outside the scope of your policy.

MARY:

But what is our policy?

FRED:

I'll mail it to you next week.

CONSULTANT:

We must look at Tom's concern, and Mary's, while respecting the manager's decision to continue participating in this area. It is a truism that what did not do well last year may do very well this year. As a firm, we judge managers on total return over a market cycle.

MARY:

What is a market cycle?

CONSULTANT:

Unfortunately, the definition is not precise, but a market cycle generally coincides with an economic cycle, a period commencing with the renewal of growth after a recession and ending when gross national product stops declining in a recession. Individual asset classes have cycles as well.

FRED:

Should we relate our investment policy to spending plans of the university?

MARY:

This is an interesting question. I have researched minutes of the board of trustees since 1985 but could not find any references to investment policy, powers delegated to this committee, points of view of previous investment committees, or reasons why we hired the manager and the consultant. I would feel more comfortable about my role and responsibilities if I could see those documents.

JOE:

Of course, Mary. You have a point. I remember those meetings well. Fred, what did we do with those records?

FRED:

I will mail you a copy of the investment policy, Mary, and I believe I have an old file concerning the manager and consultant selection process. I remember it clearly because we interviewed over 15 firms in less than two days, a real marathon.

CONSULTANT:

I remember it too, because we were so nervous and wanted to make a good impression. It was a difficult job for all involved, but this does remind me that we should again look at your investment policy to be sure that it is up to date and meets the current needs of the university. Our staff will work with you on this. Also, I want to point out the 20-page appendix to your performance booklet that describes your new method of making comparisons. We have established for you a new index that is a combination of other indexes, in other words, a standard constructed more closely to the reality of your account.

JOE:

Did I authorize that work?

CONSULTANT:

It is part of our permanent obligation to clients.

JOE:

It is getting late, and I must catch a flight home in about 90 minutes. Can we bring this meeting to a conclusion?

FRED:

I think we should spend a few minutes talking about our bond portfolio.

MARY:

It would help me to learn about the bond portfolio. Why do we have so much money in bonds when stocks have done so much better?

CONSULTANT:

Two years ago, Mary, the committee adopted a balanced approach to endowment management utilizing ideas from modern portfolio theory, which describes an "efficient" portfolio, a blend of stocks and bonds believed to provide highest return at lowest risk. The mixture mandated by this committee was 60 percent bonds, 40 percent stocks.

MARY:

Page 4 of your report says the blend is 45 percent bonds, 55 percent stocks.

CONSULTANT:

That's because stocks have had higher total returns than bonds. Since they have grown faster, their percentage of the total has increased.

MARY:

So we are not following our policy?

TOM:

That's right, and the manager is buying stocks that do not fit our policy.

MARY:

Which part of the policy?

TOM:

The requirement to avoid speculation.

CONSULTANT:

Joe, do we need to deal with these concerns? We've been doing some work on governance recently. We feel it is important to deal directly with the concerns of everyone involved. Perhaps we should have an open meeting for everyone to express their ideas.

JOE:

Let's talk about that, but I've got to leave soon. Does the committee have any more questions? It already is five o'clock. Fred, do you think you could help Mary and Tom? They both have important questions. We also need to prepare a report to the board of trustees. We'll get that done, of course.

OK. Fine. Thank you all very much. Our next meeting will be called for the third Saturday following the end of our fiscal year. I will advise you as to the time and place. See you then.

*   *   *   *   *

Joe Franklin was tired. But he had done his part. He had brought people together for a full and frank discussion, and the manager was staying within guidelines.

Tom might have a point about savings and loans, he thought, but my friend who runs an S&L told me he thinks the time is right to buy. I've got to help Mary because she doesn't have the background for this work. Maybe my investment department can send her some recent literature.

*   *   *   *   *

During the short drive home, Fred remembered that he must find policy documents to send to Mary, who was very interested, though somewhat naive about the investment process. He also wondered if the committee ever would address his concerns. But those concerns probably are not important, he thought, because the university is financially healthy. Then his mind turned toward Monday, when he must meet with student journalists, sign payroll checks, speak to the auditor, pay the president's travel voucher, review applications for bookstore manager, be sure the buildings and grounds staff was ready for graduation day, and give some thought to preparation of next year's budget.

*   *   *   *   *

Tom was frustrated. Why am I on this committee? he wondered. They have absolutely no interest in my ideas. The manager has not done well, but nobody cares, and the consultant really runs things. It is not right, but I don't know what to do about it. Maybe Joe has been doing this too long, but no one is going to ask him to resign. He's just too powerful. Should I speak to the board chairman about this? No. That would not do any good. Just cause problems. Maybe we need more people on this committee. Someone told me the perfect committee size is eight, and we have only three, plus Fred for staff input, but the professionals also are part of the committee, in a way. Anyway, three or four is supposed to be bad because one person easily dominates, while 10 more more is cumbersome. Maybe I should propose that we add new members? I'll think about it.

* * * * *

"How was it?" asked Jim.

"Lousy," said Mary. "This committee does not have its act together.

"It's very odd. Privately, every person on the committee could make a contribution. They are the brightest people I've ever met. Joe is known as a superb company administrator, while Tom has an outstanding record serving individual investors, and Fred, the controller, is in line for a promotion because he keeps things moving without offending anyone. I'm also extremely impressed with our advisors, but when we get together, nothing happens.

"There were several proposals. Someone said savings and loan stocks were bad, but we didn't vote on it. Another said we should reconcile earnings and spending, but there was no action. Another said we should revise the investment policy, but we left with no plan to do so. Tom looked frustrated to me, and Fred's concerns were not discussed. We just sat and listened, though come to think of it, I don't remember anyone taking minutes. We're running over $100 million, which scares me, and I'm confused about what my philosophy should be. We had no printed agenda, no advance reading material from the consultant, no minutes of past meetings, and no copies of governing documents. Then, after the meeting, the consultant tells me privately that I must learn about measures of portfolio risk such as standard deviation and beta, and I should know about bond quality and duration, in effect saying that I don't know what I'm doing, which is probably right. Then he proposed I attend a week-long course sponsored by his firm that would cost either me or the university over $2,000. Is this right? I'm not a dumb person, but they speak down to me. This is ridiculous. I don't want this. I want to accomplish, not just sit like a spectator at a movie. What should I do? Should I quit?"

"Tell you what," said Jim. "Let's rent a movie and relax. Would you prefer to watch *Turner and Hooch,* or *The Bonfire of the Vanities?*

* * * * *

John and Doris flew home. It should have been a good day, they thought, but it was long and unsatisfying. They did not converse about business, for it was Saturday night, time to think about family and friends, but they could not remove anxiety from their minds, an uncertainty about how they should act in the future, or whether the committee trusted them.

Are we truly part of this team, they wondered, or are we just hired hands, objects of scrutiny and criticism? They should realize we want to go in the same direction they do, but what is that direction? Are we really doing what they want us to do?

CHAPTER 5

COMMITTEES AND INVESTORS

Usually a committee is a group of people separated by a common goal.

Gene Perret, Funny Business

When an effective investor meets a capable committee, both are annoyed. Individuals challenged by personal goals, working alone without need to compromise, produce great results in athletics, music, literature, art, and investing—but it requires committees to administer great organizations. It is a dichotomy worth examining.

Author/investor John Train has studied outstanding money managers since the mid-1950s and has written several hundred columns for *The Wall Street Journal, Forbes, The New York Times,* and other publications. As president of Train, Smith Counsel in New York, Train himself has an enviable investment record. Former U.S. Senator Claiborne Pell had this to say in 1980:

> I should reveal at the outset that in addition to being a client of John Train's firm I am his cousin, and so perhaps not a completely disinterested commentator.
>
> Still, I can attest that he picks winners. The investment pool which his firm maintains and of which I am a part has risen more than seven times since the beginning of 1975, compared to two and a half times for the Dow Jones Industrial Average.[1]

Two of John Train's books are *The Money Masters* (1980) and *The New Money Masters* (1989). They both provide biographies of great investors, individuals who have proven track records, such as T. Rowe Price, Benjamin Graham, John Templeton, John Neff, and Peter Lynch. What do these and other fine investors have in common? According to John Train, each great investor "seems to have certain traits":

1. He is realistic.
2. He is intelligent to the point of genius; or else.
3. He is utterly dedicated to his craft.
4. He is disciplined and patient.
5. He is a *loner.*[2] (Emphasis added.)

Train also makes the following comparison:

> How can it be that a single individual, virtually without a staff, and managing an enormous mass of capital—the $10-billion Magellan Fund—greatly outperforms a large, able organization—the best that the governing body of an old and famous institution can assemble—handling only a fraction as much money? That is, how does Peter Lynch do so much better than his neighbors at Harvard Management?

Then Train answers his own question:

> The chief reason is that a supremely capable individual—and Peter Lynch is one—easily outmaneuvers a large committee, which essentially describes Harvard Management. Wellington, who never lost a battle, also never held councils of war; Napoleon liked to say that one general was enough for an army. In other words, the trick in those two competitive games, investment and war, is to find the ablest chief available and, under philosophical guidance, give him his head.[3]

In the context of this book, Train's statement could be misleading. His goal was to highlight the skills of Peter Lynch by comparing him to another professional investment organization, Harvard Management, which itself has achieved respectable returns by managing money internally. However, the purpose of this is to alert trustees to the differences between needs of their investment committees and the personal needs of outstanding professional investors. Money managers value independence, while investment committees value accountability.

Train's money masters manage wealth held by individuals, partnerships, or mutual funds. These owners are different from retirement plans, endowments, and foundations. The differences, outlined in Table 4–1, are important.

These differences begin to explain the dynamics of committee/investor relationships. Retirement plans and nonprofits are active owners that write policies and enforce restrictions on both techniques and specific investments. Investment committees of these plan sponsors tend to be very concerned that all decisions are appropriate for a specific institutional culture or perceived legal requirements. In contrast, a mutual fund manager can work alone. The fund's owners seldom influence investment policy. Within policy constraints described in a prospectus, a mutual fund manager can make decisions independently. Since most individuals prefer to work unfettered, there is an inherent cultural

---

TABLE 4–1
Differences between Plan Sponsors

Retirement Plans, Foundations, and Endowments	Individuals, Private Partnerships, and Mutual Funds*
Tax free	Taxable
Capital belongs to others (beneficiaries)	Individuals own most capital
Founded on consensus	Self-directed, private, and personal
Fiduciary responsibility under law	Fewer legal obligations
Traditionally managed by committees	Traditionally managed by individuals
Comfortable with large investment firms and consultants that themselves manage by consensus	Comfortable with independent, creative investment managers having wide discretion
More interested in public service or retirement benefits than investing	Exclusively dedicated to investing
Managers visit clients in person	Managers usually do not know owners personally
Managers have fewer clients; they are more directly accountable	Managers work for thousands of investors

*Mutual funds do serve investors in the first column, but at a distance. A retirement plan, for example, would be only one of thousands of investors in a mutual fund.

---

mismatch between the committee decision-making process and the personalized, individual, creative needs of professional investors.

This dichotomy, this clash of action styles between a committee and an individual, illustrates both the art of investing and the nature of a committee. Often a great investor is uncomfortable with the demands of a committee, the overwhelming need for explicit goals and precise guidelines built from compromise, while a committee feels distressed upon giving total authority and discretion to one person or one company without contractual restrictions derived from the committee's sense of prudence. The investor seeks independence; the committee requires support of many personalities and viewpoints.

But as trustees we must respect the committee system. It is the central nervous system of most organizations directed by trustees. Unlike investing, the delivery of tangible goods and services always requires compromise in the creation of policy and goals, as well as cooperation in their execution. Though it is feasible to assign investment responsibility to one person, it is not possible for a single individual to produce and distribute a significant product or service. This can be done only through an organization managed by committees. Inevitably, one of these is the investment committee. It must hear and respect many ideas. Its decision-making process is democratic, compassionate, and sensitive to many different interests. Effective investment committees work hard to achieve consensus.

The real needs of an organization—financial stability and asset growth—demand resolution of the temperamental mismatch between professional investors and committees. Trustees can improve the relationship—and achieve superior rates of return—by looking carefully at themselves. Trustees allocate capital effectively when they understand the nature of a committee and design an efficient method to make and implement decisions. In seeking efficiency, however, a committee should avoid common pitfalls, such as the following:

1. Absence of a written statement of strategic goals by the parent organization, leaving each investment committee trustee only an ambiguous personal view of the future.
2. Ambiguity about authority. Can the committee make final decisions, or must the full board decide? Over which decisions does the committee have full discretion?
3. Limited time at points of significant change, such as when new trustees join the committee or when the committee must hire new professional advisors. In these circumstances, a committee seldom meets long enough to consider each member's concerns; issues always remain for further study. Some participants feel like spectators at a basketball game that their team would have won if there had been 10 more seconds.
4. Too much time dedicated for routine meetings such as performance reviews. These are only listening sessions. No new policies are proposed. Brief telephone conference calls are sufficient.
5. Failure to identify beneficiaries or owners. For whom are we working? Today's students or tomorrow's? Members of the association or its corporate sponsors? The company or its employees?
6. Inadequate training of new trustees.

7. Omission of traditional meeting procedures, such as advance circulation of reports, proposals, and agendas, as well as failure to recognize and respect rules of order. Every day, meetings rush to obscurity by allowing proposals without seconds, questions-turned-into-speeches, and long debates about when to have the next meeting.

8. Control by a minority of one or two who are perceived as experts or have served a long time.

9. Confusion about staff and volunteer responsibilities, which may engender feelings of uselessness among volunteers and insecurity among staff.

The committee that surmounts these obstacles is prepared to meet its investment responsibilities. In the following chapters, this book tries to help.

NOTES

1. John Train, *The Money Masters* (New York: Harper & Row, 1980), p. ix.
2. Ibid., p. 213.
3. John Train, *The New Money Masters* (New York: Harper & Row, 1989), p. 192.

CHAPTER 6

UNDERSTANDING INVESTMENTS: DEBT AND EQUITY— PERCEPTION AND REALITY

Neither a borrower nor a lender be.

Polonius to Laertes, in Shakespeare's Hamlet

Everyone has attitudes about debt and equity. Polonius, like many 20th-century fathers, opposed personal debt as a matter of character (though we do not know his thoughts about business debt). Politicians espouse the evils of public debt, and many state constitutions prohibit borrowing. Normally, retirement plans and trust accounts may not borrow, an imprudent act in most fiduciary relationships, but they are allowed—even encouraged—to lend.

Equity also has detractors, those who see intolerable volatility in stock prices and real estate values. To some, equity investments are mysterious, part of a private activity pursued only by insiders, institutions, brilliant theoreticians, and the strong of heart. At one extreme is the Indiana attorney general who declared that state retirement funds may not acquire equity securities, a ruling subsequently affirmed by two state-wide referenda. In that state, more than 50 percent of the voters feel there is something wrong with equities, and therefore debt is the only acceptable investment. (However, Indiana is one of only two states to prohibit equities, and most states have been steadily increasing their equity holdings in recent years.)

Debt and equity are more than financial concepts. They evoke attitudes and feelings, apprehensions or excitement. Investors comprehend these two elements of investment capital but also feel an emotion, a moral sensitivity that one is good or bad, while the other is attractive, useful, or practical, a necessary component of a smart investment program. It is the same with nations. To the casual observer, other nations have images and ethical values, but seasoned diplomats, political scientists, and historians, see only states to be evaluated, measured, and occasionally manipulated.

To allocate funds effectively, trustees must be like diplomats and historians. They must view debt and equity through impartial, objective eyes that see only tangible connections to the productive capacities of society.

The purpose of this chapter is to prove that modern investment securities and their many derivatives—such as options, warrants, and futures contracts—were born of a genuine economic need and that there is a compelling logic behind seemingly erratic changes in price. Let's start the discussion of investment terminology by reviewing the origins of an enterprise.

The first enterprise required only nature's gifts and labor. Soon it expanded, and it needed tools, research, distribution, management, and cooperation. Cooperation appeared in two forms. The first was teamwork. The second was capital.

Capital is all of the resources provided by those who can benefit from the enterprise, such as managers, suppliers, customers, and investors seeking a return. Among the massive group of potential investors are trustees, who want only a positive return on the funds they provide in the form of debt (lending) and equity (owning). *Debt* and *equity* are simple to define but hard to understand, for while they elicit concepts in the mind, they also evoke emotions and biases that retard progress toward understanding.

A framework for understanding investment language arises from historical changes in the perception of debt and equity. When I was a child in the 1950s, my parents took pride in their debt-free lifestyle (100 percent equity in home and car). Like Benjamin Franklin, they lectured about the dangers of borrowing, but they also recommended U.S. savings bonds and savings accounts as solid, conservative investments. In other words, they were proud to lend, but not to borrow; they did not recognize an inconsistency between their opinion of borrowing and their willingness to help borrowers by depositing personal funds with lenders. While they felt a lender (depositor, bondholder) was wise, the borrower was foolish. Today, there are similarly inconsistent attitudes about government financing because investors criticize Uncle Sam for deficit spending while simultaneously declaring that Treasury bills, notes, and bonds are the most conservative investments available. These investors support an evil they criticize.

Perceptions of investment terms changed in the 1960s for at least three reasons:

1. The end of depression and war brought about better markets and greater personal comfort with stocks.
2. The income tax structure favored capital gains.
3. Increasing inflation prompted greater interest in growth securities.

Books and magazines began to encourage personal borrowing, especially to own real estate. Charismatic public speakers with powerful, resonant voices argued that the best way to get rich was to borrow and invest. Acquiring a home and a car by incurring debt became socially acceptable, but it was socially unacceptable to place personal savings in banks and bonds. Investors boasted about their portfolios of common stocks, which, of course, are equities, while remaining silent about their acquisition of debt securities. Investor psychology of the 1960s was the reverse of that of the 1950s; the earlier 100 percent owner of a home who saved in banks and bonds now held only 30 percent equity in a mortgaged home, purchased one or two cars on four-year notes, speculated in stocks, and was ready to advise others to do the same.

The words *socially acceptable* and *socially unacceptable* are important to this discussion. They refer to conventional wisdom, beliefs expressed in social settings and popular literature. The words imply a divergence between belief and reality. In reality, investors of the 1950s had mortgages and purchased stocks, and investors of the 1960s obviously placed part of their savings in thrift institutions. However, these actions were not respected in the literature or in casual discourse. Investors who acquired stocks in the 1950s didn't tell anyone, but by the 1960s they advertised their ownership of stocks while concealing their savings accounts and bonds.

Another example of the changing fads in investment language is *junk bond,* an imprecise term (usually meaning ''below investment grade'') that has fallen from attractive to unacceptable. In the early 1980s, junk bonds, or high-yield bonds, were acceptable and exciting. Investors believed that junk bonds represented a new asset class that paid high income and appreciated in value. Investors spoke well of their skill in acquiring junk bonds. By the end of the decade, however, high-yield junk bonds were associated with numerous defaults and dramatic declines in market value, with the inevitable result that investors no longer were proud to own them and did not discuss them favorably. The term *junk bond,* therefore, evolved from positive to negative in less than 10 years. (While *junk bond* appeared to attract, then discourage, amateur investors, the more precise term, *low-rated* or *nonrated security,* maintained a stable definition and image, demonstrating that correct terms are more useful and less likely to mislead.)

Contemporary connotations of investment terms such as *junk bond, debt,* and *equity* influence actions of both individuals and investment committees. Conventional wisdom has special power over committees that do not want to diverge too far from their peers, constituents, and

U.S. Individuals' Financial Portfolio

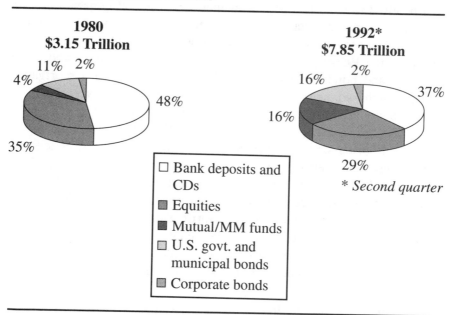

Just as skirt lengths change, investment assets and techniques gain and lose popularity over time. For example, individual and institutional ownership of common stocks increased significantly from 1950 to 1970. Some reliable recent data chronicles preference changes between 1980 and 1992. Individuals (a category that includes nonprofits) owned more bank deposits and CDs in 1980 than in 1992, but four times as many mutual funds in 1992 than in 1980. Public pension funds almost doubled their ownership of equities, while life insurance companies reduced equities and increased U.S. government securities.

Mutual Funds' Financial Portfolio

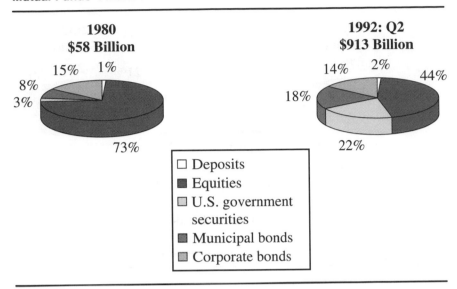

1980
$58 Billion

1992: Q2
$913 Billion

□ Deposits
■ Equities
□ U.S. government
   securities
■ Municipal bonds
□ Corporate bonds

Private Pension Funds' Financial Portfolio

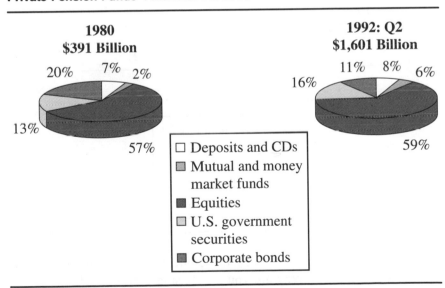

1980
$391 Billion

1992: Q2
$1,601 Billion

□ Deposits and CDs
□ Mutual and money
   market funds
■ Equities
□ U.S. government
   securities
■ Corporate bonds

beneficiaries. If everyone believes the world is flat, it takes courage to argue publicly that it is round because at least one listener will think the advocate is absolutely crazy. An investment committee can see potential

Public Pension Funds' Financial Portfolio

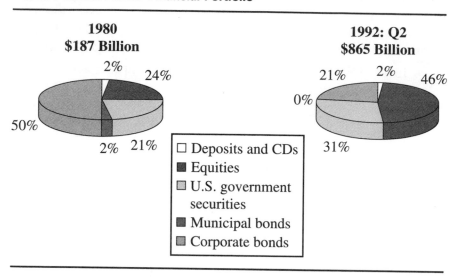

1980
$187 Billion

2%   24%

21%

50%

2%   21%

☐ Deposits and CDs
■ Equities
▨ U.S. government
   securities
■ Municipal bonds
▨ Corporate bonds

1992: Q2
$865 Billion

21%   2%   46%

0%

31%

Foreign Financial Portfolio

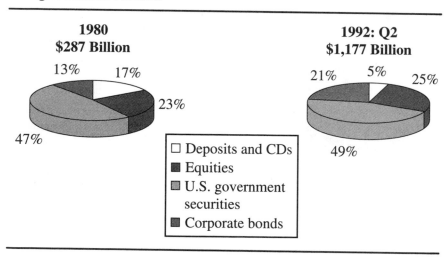

1980
$287 Billion

13%   17%

23%

47%

☐ Deposits and CDs
■ Equities
▨ U.S. government
   securities
■ Corporate bonds

1992: Q2
$1,177 Billion

21%   5%   25%

49%

in low-rated or nonrated debt securities, but it will avoid them because observers might ask, "Why are you purchasing junk bonds?"

The popular belief of the 1950s was that bonds and high-dividend stocks were more prudent investments than growth stocks. Although individuals were acquiring growth stocks privately, few were willing to propose them for large funds because at least one other trustee was bound to say, "This is crazy!" (Translation: "You are crazy!")

Life Insurance Companies' Financial Portfolio

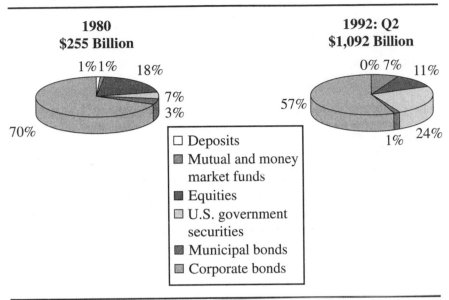

1980
$255 Billion

1992: Q2
$1,092 Billion

□ Deposits
■ Mutual and money
   market funds
■ Equities
▨ U.S. government
   securities
■ Municipal bonds
▨ Corporate bonds

Conventional wisdom and implicit definitions of investment terms especially influenced college and university endowments, perhaps because large boards govern these institutions and several constituencies aggressively deliver advice (boards of visitors, alumni associations, faculty congresses, and student newspapers). A relevant hypothesis may be this: The larger the board and the more prominent its members, the slower it is to change. A business, cultural, or academic leader does not want to risk his or her professional image by proposing new methods that seem radical to a larger audience. In fact, endowments adopted modern investment thinking in the late 1960s, at least 10 years behind the times, only because the Ford Foundation used both carrot and stick to encourage change. The carrot was scholarly commentary:

> The record of most American colleges and universities in increasing the value of their endowments through investment management has not been good. . . . We believe the fundamental reason is that trustees of most educational institutions, because of their semipublic character, have applied a special standard of prudence to endowment management which places primary emphasis on avoiding losses and maximizing present income. Thus, the possibility that other goals might be reasonable—and perhaps preferable—has hardly been considered.[1]

Other Insurance Companies' Financial Portfolio

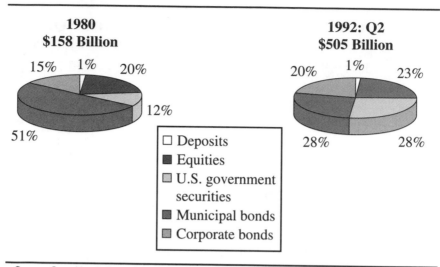

1980
$158 Billion

15%   1%   20%

12%

51%

1992: Q2
$505 Billion

20%   1%   23%

28%   28%

□ Deposits
■ Equities
□ U.S. government
   securities
■ Municipal bonds
□ Corporate bonds

Source: Securities Industry Association, "Changing Institutional Investment Patterns," December 14, 1992.

The stick was an implied threat that more grants would go to institutions that adopted the foundation's point of view. This powerful message directly challenged the conventional wisdom of trustees while giving them a tool to change. It said, in effect, "We think you have been too conservative, too fearful of loss, and you can use our words to support new investment policies without fear of losing personal prestige because if it does not work out, it is our fault, not yours." The battle was against a "special standard of prudence," an anxiety about equity born of the debacles of the 1930s but totally out of date by the late 1960s, when individuals were willing to acquire growth securities but trustees were not. They could accurately define *equity, growth,* and *maximum long-term return,* but they could not as trustees meeting in committee arrive at a consensual understanding and acceptance, the prerequisites for change.

The 1970s and 1980s will be known more for the introduction of new terms than for changes in the definitions of old ones. During these years, managing data by computer gave both experts and amateurs greater understanding of historic price changes. Thus, terms like *beta* and *standard deviation,* both measures of risk and volatility, gained wider acceptance and credibility. Words describing relationships within a portfolio, such as *covariance,* were used more frequently, but the greatest contribution to investment language was *asset allocation,* a term unknown in the 1960s that now even appears in titles of books. It represents a powerful and important concept in portfolio management.

The purpose here is not to define words, but to demonstrate that the meanings of words change and that connotations occasionally mislead. Members of effective investment committees must come both to know and to understand the language of investing by removing the emotional baggage of words, seeking definitions instead of connotations, and looking to specifics instead of generalities. It is very important that trustees understand debt and equity, the most basic financial concepts.

The search for understanding starts by observing how debt and equity facilitate the production of goods and services, while simultaneously earning a positive return for investors. This is capitalism at work, a dynamic process that requires flexibility and appreciation of risk and return. It is so simple as to deceive, especially for investors exposed to daily price changes of stocks and bonds, and the hundreds of complex theories explaining why. In the information age, it is easy to forget basic information. Hence, the following narrative is provided.

An enterprise starts with a product or idea that usually may be developed or described on paper at little cost. Implementation, however, requires tools and materials. The founder might own those resources, as the carpenter owns a hammer, but will not always have enough personal resources to grow. The founder must therefore obtain financing from others by issuing equity, debt, or both.

To illustrate, a certain company that produces fax machines, for example, has $1 million to develop and build one bench prototype, but it needs $3 million to manufacture 5,000 machines per year. The solution is clear. In exchange for an additional $1 million invested by a board of trustees (probably indirectly), the company gives out 499 of its 1,000 shares, keeping control but promising to share profits proportionately with other equity owners. Then the company makes a deal with an investment banker to raise another $1 million in exchange for notes that promise to return the money in 10 years, paying 9 percent interest in the meantime. The company now has $3 million to purchase tools, equipment, and supplies.

In its first year, the company produces and sells 5,000 fax machines, creating a net profit of $400,000 after paying all operating expenses, interest on debt, and taxes. This equates to 40 cents' profit for each of the

1 million shares outstanding. Assuming that the original $3 million was invested in assets still having a market value of $3 million, the company now is worth $3.4 million, unless, of course, some of the profit is paid to owners in cash as a common dividend. If not, the company has $400,000 more this year than last, and it can purchase another machine, perhaps increasing the production of fax machines from 5,000 to 10,000, doubling the profit. As each year passes, the common shareholders (equity owners) receive benefits of this growth through dividends and increased net worth, while owners of bonds (debt) can be increasingly confident their money will be returned in full on the maturity date.

Trustees, this you must know—and understand—to be effective: Growth will accrue on the capital you invest for others, and debt will be repaid, as long as enterprises earn profits. While consultants talk past performance, money managers present investment styles and techniques, professors describe modern portfolio theory, and investment bankers create variations of debt and equity, never forget the connection to production and profit!

Thousands of enterprises operate with capital raised through hundreds of different forms of debt and equity, described by words such as *warrants, options, pass throughs, collateralized, guaranteed, long, short, notes, bonds, bills, convertibles, preferreds,* and a host of others that make investing seem complex. Meanwhile, theoreticians and corporate finance specialists have studied, thought, planned, and calculated, striving to make sense out of thousands of different securities and hundreds of thousands of different possible combinations of securities in portfolios. Consultants have created theoretical categories such as income or growth, small cap or large cap, conservative or speculative, emerging or emerged. These analysts have observed intriguing interaction among debt and equity securities and their derivatives. They hypothesize that trustees can eliminate risks of a single company or industry by combining some assets with other assets in large portfolios, leaving only the risks of the market and of society itself. Finally, they have proved the classic assumption that potential returns are related to the magnitude of risk assumed, a surprise indeed.

It is not essential to understand every theory and definition. Professional pilots can fly planes as long as passengers trust flying itself. Yet the joy of investing increases for trustees who know and love the words and language, the concepts and strategies, the certainties and uncertainties.

Comprehension gives comfort. Trustees who visualize macroeconomic effects of their decisions are more likely to make appropriate decisions and less likely to feel any misleading apprehensions. Hiring a money manager and accepting an investment style are merely ways to build pipelines between the investment committee and productive enterprises. One line is debt, the other equity, and the committee can choose which is most appropriate for a given circumstance.

The trustee's obligations are (1) to understand the charmingly simple growth process facilitated by debt and equity and (2) to recognize and eliminate the emotional content of investment language arising from popular literature and conventional wisdom. A further task is to create a collective understanding in which the investment committee, or even the entire board of trustees, has insight, objectivity, flexibility, and willingness to innovate—a state of efficiency recognized by professional observers when they can say, "That committee knows what it is doing; it understands the art of investing."

NOTE

1. From Charles D. Ellis and James R. Vertin, the Ford Foundation, "The Problem; the Approach," quoted in *Classics, an Investor's Anthology,* Homewood, Ill.: Business One Irwin, 1989), pp. 366–67.

CHAPTER 7

RELATIONSHIP OF THE BOARD PROCESS TO THE INVESTMENT PROCESS

All paths lead to the same goal: to convey to others what we are. And we must pass through solitude and difficulty, isolation and silence, in order to reach forth to the enchanted place where we can dance our clumsy dance and sing our sorrowful song—but in this dance or in this song there are fulfilled the most ancient rites of our conscience in the awareness of being human and of believing in a common destiny.

Pablo Neruda

Ideally, trustees establish goals and then delegate their implementation to staff or outside advisors. However, it is more difficult to create investment goals than any other form of board policy. The difficulty is related to the intangible nature and perceived volatility of many investment assets. One legitimately might ask, "How can we establish specific and measurable goals for an activity that seems to lack both consistency and predictability?"

To create goals that connect investment results to organizational functions, boards first distinguish between personal and organizational objectives. Then they distinguish means from ends. Finally, they learn to predict and tolerate risk.

Let's start with the personal. One person points in pride to his status as governor, while another says simply, "I built a highway." The first is head of a state and appears self-satisfied with a title, but the second, who may be a political leader, engineer, or worker, cites his accomplishment before his title. This person worked in cooperation with hundreds of others to create a lasting benefit that can be seen, touched, and appreciated.

Between these two persons, the difference is at once obvious and subtle. Presumably, a governor achieves one personal goal by being elected, but citizens naturally hope that their governor also wants to encourage progress toward tangible ends such as health care and new highways. In fact, an exemplary candidate runs for governor *only* because he or she has specific, concrete objectives most effectively pursued as head of state, and voters hope to remember the governor's accomplishments more than his or her arrival at high office. We want to remember elected officials by what they do for us.

Like voters watching public leaders, observers of organizations want tangible results. They want to see and feel accomplishments. As either participants in or beneficiaries of an organization, observers say, "Get something done. Help me, my friends, or my family. I want positive results!"

It follows that a trustee should determine what to achieve (a personal agenda) by defining important ends. Effective trustees have a personal vision that guides their actions and governs what initiatives they propose. Meanwhile, the board should decide what to do for its beneficiaries while distinguishing means from ends. The job is not to write policy, to allocate assets, or to measure performance. It is not to hire money managers or to talk frequently with consultants, and it is not to reduce costs. The important tasks are to deliver positive investment results and to avoid unacceptable risks.

Accomplishments arise from vision. Trustees need vision, a belief that they and their organization are headed in a specific direction that is likely to produce a positive, concrete result. They must feel like part of a team as they work in some small way to contribute to the exciting consummation foreseen by the team. Their individual role might be to lead the entire organization or to develop policy for a department or function, such as managing the investment portfolio, but whatever the role, a trustee needs to accept a vision and facilitate progress toward a specific and measurable goal.

Establishing goals for investments is a peculiar process for two reasons. First, successful investing is less the result of human exertion than of being in the right place at the right time. Additional labor does not produce proportionately better results, and American ideas about developing skill through practice, taking part in personal competition (especially athletic competition), and working additional hours to produce more product do not apply. The person who sets an investment goal cannot assure himself that extra exertion will help him reach that goal. Second, trusteed investments usually are intangibles (stocks, bonds, and their derivatives) that represent reality but are not themselves palpable. Therefore, making a transition from the real world of measured production and sales to the intangible world of "total return," "duration," "efficient frontiers" and "200-day moving averages" may be difficult. It generates culture shock, an abrupt change without preparation, a disbelief like that the audience feels during the first few minutes of an animated Walt Disney film.

The tangible and intangible worlds might seem so different that trustees fail to see a connection between the two. What is the connection, for example, between investments of a retirement plan and the products of a company? What is the connection between the advanced education of 2,000 students and a college's investment portfolio? What is the real relationship between the investment return on a $1 billion endowment and the endowment's community efforts? When trustees meet during an economic or market crisis, fear and indecision can overwhelm vision, especially if the vision itself is not clear, if the only item on their true agenda is to avoid loss. In this circumstance, trustees might rashly decide to invest only in asset classes perceived to have less risk, and they might fail to consider the missed opportunity costs of a timid investment policy. It would be easy for their collective mind to forget that their fundamental mission is to educate students (today's and tomorrow's), or to alleviate poverty, or to build a museum, or to pay retirement benefits, both now and in the future.

It is equally easy for an investment committee to believe that writing a policy and hiring a money manager are achievements, but they are not. They are road signs, not destinations. "People tend to become so engrossed in activity," said one commentator, "that they lose sight of its purpose. . . . They become so enmeshed in activity they lose sight of why they are doing it, and the activity becomes a false goal, an end in itself."[1]

Instead, investment committees should seek accomplishment in the real world, a result (according to the Atlanta Consulting Group) of inspired performance that "is no accident. Outstanding organizational results become possible when a management or project team creates a vision of a desired future and commits to turning that vision into reality by instituting the goals, structures, and systems to support its attainment."[2] Vision connects investment decisions and real projects. It gives perspective.

The vision should be expressed in a statement written by an entire board of trustees that becomes both a motivator and a kind of fiber-optic telephone line between the board and its committees. It is an aspiration shared by all trustees and all board committees. Trustees should express their vision in the present tense, as do athletes who whisper to themselves, "I am winning," instead of, "I am going to win."

Vision statements are personal, somewhat corny, and general, often suggesting high ideals seemingly beyond reach, as though they emanate from philosophers who promise a new world order of peace and tranquility. The following are two actual examples:

> We are a loving, supportive team of top professionals. We empower people to create organizations with vision, harmony, commitment and inspired results. Integrity and dealing from the heart are our highest values. Our work is fun and exciting and brings wealth, respect, and joy in abundance for us and the people we touch.[3]

> We are an inspired team dedicated to achieving the highest quality of life through health care. We are individuals united by our commitment to the human values of honor, respect, trust and personal growth for all people. We create success by doing it right.[4]

The next examples are hypothetical:

- We are dedicated retirement plan trustees who provide our colleagues a safe and secure future, with few financial concerns. We are committed to constantly improving our understanding of investments by continuous self-study and close, amiable working relationships with professional investment advisors.
- Our community foundation is helping to develop infrastructure and programs that benefit all our neighbors. We grow individually as trustees by helping our neighbors and by improving our physical surroundings.
- This university is a special place of learning, friendship, loyalty, and trust where students, teachers, staff, and alumni grow personally through exposure to ideas and the encouragement of inquisitiveness. We are using our resources judiciously to provide a quality education. We are committed to associating with the brightest students and faculty within the most commodious, relaxed, and beautiful facilities and parks possible.

To elaborate on the importance of vision and its effect on investment committees, let's concentrate only on the hypothetical university, while asserting that the imperative is equally important for retirement plans and foundations. The purpose here will be to demonstrate that any investment committee operates best by responding to the larger purposes of the organization. The university is an excellent model because its trustees aspire to provide the best possible instruction in the most comfortable facilities available. For the sake of argument, let's assume the trustees of this university want to create the most outstanding educational institution in the world, an ambition requiring effective governance, terrific personnel—and a superb investment program. Let's further assume that the university's trustees recognize that they have adopted an extremely ambitious objective and that the road to it might have chuckholes. In other words, the trustees know they have accepted a high degree of risk.

As stated earlier, the vision statement is a prerequisite to success. It should utilize the present tense to state aspirations that may be more forcefully stated in two additional documents: the mission statement and the list of specific, measurable goals. The mission statement of the university cites general goals of achieving efficient administration, recruiting outstanding students, and raising money from alumni. Then the board provides particular goals, such as attracting first-rate faculty by paying high salaries; building particular new buildings and renovating old ones; and funding named projects in research, music, and the arts. The list of specific goals also proposes building several new living units and recreational facilities, as well as expanding scholarship aid to attract students. These specific, written goals are to be achieved by stated dates with predictable costs. They have been accepted by the entire board of trustees and staff, and advertised to all constituencies. The entire university community knows where it is headed.

As members of the university's board of trustees, investment committee members accept and support the vision, mission, and goal statements because they helped create them. Now the job is to carry out an outstanding investment program that seeks superior results, more capital for buildings and grounds, and more income for operations. Like the board as a whole, the investment committee knows it is an ambitious program and that circumstances might delay its implementation, but there is a belief that the risks are worth taking. Some of the risks will be investment risks.

A TALE OF TWO POLICIES
Two Hypothetical Situations; Two Different Responses

I. HIGH RISK

University X has a stable enrollment, solid alumni support, and a $100 million endowment from two successful fund-raising campaigns during the last 10 years. During the next 10 years, its board of trustees would like to make notable improvements, including a new student union, a new science building, and a new athletic center. It also wants to spend 8 percent of endowment assets each year for operations, an amount double the maximum spending rates its consultant says will protect principal and permit growth. However, the board is persistent and has instructed the investment committee to seek above-average returns. The investment committee decides to place 50 percent of the endowment in small capitalization stocks, 25 percent in foreign securities, and 25 percent in managed futures, a mix it believes might produce stellar returns.

The committee and its consultant also prepare a risk statement that hypothesizes a 50 percent potential decline in endowment value under adverse circumstances. The board of trustees evaluates this contingency. It accepts the policy after concluding that such a decline would seriously stunt the university's growth but would not put it out of business. In other words, it agrees to the risk.

II. LOW RISK

Enrollment at college Y has been declining. Problems started six years ago when the president and faculty reached an impasse over curriculum requirements. The president resigned, and the acting president made no proposals, assuming that the board would name a new president quickly. The nationally recognized music school dean passed away without a successor, and serious music students drifted away. Also, the college's winning reputation in baseball and soccer was waning after three losing seasons. Last year, the college elected a new chairperson of the board of trustees, who, in turn, found a new and apparently popular president in less than six months. Unfortunately, during the president's first two months in office, freak fires destroyed the old main classroom building and gutted the largest dormitory, forcing students to find temporary housing in town. The board has responded by affirming its vision statement but rewriting its mission statement and strategic goals to emphasize rapid rebuilding, hiring a new music school dean and an athletic director, and providing more scholarship aid to recruit students. The college controller immediately argued that a decline in endowment value could damage the rebuilding effort. After numerous conference calls among interested parties, the investment committee writes a new policy to eliminate as much risk to principal as possible. The investment manager sells all stocks, and purchases U.S. Treasury securities with short maturities.

Table 7–1

How Pensions Allocate Their Assets (Pensions & Investments/Callan Associates)

Asset mix changes (median)	9/30/93 (expected)	9/30/92 (actual)
Stocks	55.0%	52.0%
Bonds	35.0	37.0
Cash	3.0	4.0
Real estate	5.8	5.0
Other	1.2	2.0

Median allocations to alternatives (for those currently using)

Indexed equities (median)	15%	14%
Passive fixed income (median)	15	15.35
International equities	9	7
International fixed	5	2.6
Mortgages	4	5
Mortgage-backed securities	8	6
Internally managed equities	10	12
Internally managed fixed	17	23

Percent of executives currently using or interested in:

Passive currency hedging	24.4%
Active currency hedging	45.2
Market neutral portfolios	42.8
Tactical asset allocation	44.8
Derivatives (futures/options)	58.4

Percent of executives planning manager changes:	*Planning to hire*	*Planning to drop*
Core value equity	14.4%	11.6%
Core growth equity	12.8	7.2
Small cap growth	17.2	6.0
International equity	24.0	4.8
International fixed	9.6	0.4
Domestic fixed	11.2	5.2
Real estate equity	7.2	5.2

Courtesy, Pensions & Investments.

The practical manifestation of vision is *asset allocation,* the distribution of capital to different types of investments. Trustees who require more future resources to implement their vision take on greater risks in hopes of greater rewards. Tables 7–1 and 7–2 provide average data from many plan sponsors.

Table 7-2

How Foundations Allocate Their Assets, 1992.

	By Type of Foundation			By Size of Foundation				
	Independent and Private Operating	Community	Corporate	Under $10,000,000	$10,000,000 to $49,999,999	$50,000,000 to $99,999,999	$100,000,000 and over	All
Average portfolio composition								
Domestic stock	47.6%	28.2%	19.4%	31.3%	42.9%	39.4%	52.5%	38.8%
Foreign stock	2.4	1.4	0.3	1.0	2.7	2.2	2.9	1.9
Bonds	33.9	37.4	39.3	35.6	35.9	36.1	31.3	35.0
Cash	9.1	21.5	31.5	22.2	10.4	17.0	6.1	15.8
Real estate	2.8	1.2	1.0	2.3	2.7	1.0	2.2	2.2
Program-related investments	0.2	0.1	0.1	0.2	0.2	0.1	0.1	0.2
Pooled funds	3.3	9.8	6.7	6.8	4.8	3.1	4.0	5.4
Other	0.6	0.4	1.8	0.6	0.4	1.1	0.9	0.6
Manage some assets internally	37.9	34.2	57.4	45.6	31.4	36.3	38.3	39.4
Average percentage of assets managed internally	70.9	67.1	90.1	83.8	66.6	61.9	53.6	73.1
Regularly hire external asset managers	72.6	54.6	35.2	54.7	76.2	64.8	67.5	63.9

Reprinted with permission of *The Chronicle of Philanthropy.*

SUGGESTIONS

The investment committee should consider the following suggestions for implementing an outstanding investment program.

1. Act now! Lost time is lost money. (See Chapter 12, Table 12–1, p. 111, entitled "The Cost of Delay.")

2. Seek empowerment. The investment committee should be composed of members of the board of trustees who can effectively gain board authority to act. There should be no question in the minds of any trustee that the investment committee has the right to make final, binding decisions.

3. Create a unique, aggressive investment policy, and explain the policy to the board. Request reproduction of the investment policy in minutes of the board. Maintain records of all debate leading to creation of the policy, including disagreements.

4. Compel the board of a nonprofit to have a spending policy, also reproduced in the minutes. Be sure there is consensus, or at least an agreement, about how much income is required from endowment capital to cover operating expenses. The board should hear every constituency, especially committees on budget, finance, and buildings and grounds, as well as the faculty and staff. Though it may be impractical to have a joint meeting of all parties, it is feasible either to have conference telephone calls among committee chairs or to circulate draft policies for written comment. There should be no attempt, direct or implied, to keep this discussion confidential. Even alums with pet projects should be heard. To be heard is to support.

5. Schedule sufficient meeting time to reach consensus. Circulate the agenda in advance, and use time efficiently. Try to avoid fatigue.

6. At least once every five years, meet at a relaxed, remote location for more visioning, brainstorming, and trustee training. Include plenty of time for recreation, good food, and rest.

7. Prepare a crisis action plan. Trustees must know how to act during major market changes.

8. Professional investors prefer to be at their desks, making decisions and studying markets. Trustees prefer to create. Therefore, schedule a minimum number of meetings and present new ideas at each one.

9. Understand risk. Investment committees should accept the possibility of loss and the probability of temporary declines. Just as the fear of crowds discourages some people from attending great concerts and sporting events, fear of loss inhibits actions and restrains innovation.

Committees and boards should talk openly about risk and should predict the magnitude of possible loss under adverse circumstances. In so doing, the committee and board will become comfortable with more aggressive portfolio strategies.

10. Determine the costs and opportunities of taking on risk. What is the *real* effect if a $100 million endowment declines to $90 million, or if an $80,000 foundation is reduced to $55,000? If the practical effect is minimal, take the risk. If it is disastrous, avoid it. (See the box, "A Tale of Two Policies.")

11. Quantify goals and monitor results. In classic investment parlance, the terms *goals* and *results* have narrow meanings. For example, an investment goal might be "to earn a total rate of return that exceeds the inflation rate by 5 percent" or "to earn more than the S&P 500 Index in three out of every five years." On the other hand, an organizational goal might be to build a new library in five years or to increase retirement benefits by a stated amount. The first expression is relative, the second concrete. Similarly, classic reporting of investment results provides statements of total return and comparisons to indexes or other, similar institutional investment accounts. Again, these reports are relative. Concrete results are a newly built library or increased retirement benefits. This suggestion proposes that trustees set concrete, real-world objectives, such as "The goal of investment fund A is to construct a library in five years" or "Investment fund B will grow to provide an additional $1 million of annual scholarship assistance by 1999." Of course, writing these goal statements requires rate-of-return assumptions, but the new method of expression assures greater symmetry between investment activities and real programs. It is goal creation that inherently requires cooperation between different groups influencing organizational governance. Logically, it also insists that staffs of organizations and professional investment consultants modify their performance reports to include real accomplishments (e.g., "The library was built. Now, what is your next objective?"). (Most consultants compare results to indexes and peer groups, a limiting procedure. What difference does it make if the university is earning more or less than the S&P 500, or is beating the average of all small colleges? Arbitrary national averages do not an institution make.)

12. Cultivate outstanding rapport with professional advisors. The professional who feels threatened and insecure cannot provide good advice; he or she can say only what the committee wants to hear. Each trustee should sign a pledge that states, "I will not be offended by your

Table 7–3
From Goals to Investments

Nonprofit	Retirement Plan
Board of trustees writes and publishes vision.	Board of directors writes and publishes corporate vision.
Board prepares statements of mission, strategic goals.	Investment committee writes its mission.
Investment committee proposes risk statement to board.	Board, committee, and actuary calculate and declare minimum required returns.
Investment committee writes investment policy.	Investment committee decides amount of risk it will assume to exceed required returns.
Investment committee hires money managers.	Executives and investment committee hire money managers.
Constituents comment to board of trustees.	Beneficiaries (employees) comment to investment committee.

personal opinion if it is different from mine. I respect your expertise!'' If performance by an advisor is negative or below average, take time to evaluate the reason; give the advisor every opportunity to explain his or her decisions and why they will produce good results in the future.

13. During meetings, place the written vision and strategic goals either on the wall or in the board meeting book. Always focus on the future.

14. Limit discussion of generalities such as the economy, and promote discussion about the institution. Make professional advisors aware of their client's circumstances.

15. Clarify staff responsibilities. Consider designating one staff member to coordinate investment activities, provided he or she has both the time and the inclination. In a university setting, consider utilizing faculty and student mindpower, as well as computers and library resources, to both develop new ideas and reduce costs of administration.

16. Require self-education. Trustees who read only popular investment literature will maintain only conventional wisdom. Instead, they must read great commentaries of the past and scholarly journals of the present. Preparatory reading is especially important if the committee is going to consider innovation. Every trustee must understand details of the proposed change because the unfamiliar is speculative, while the familiar is conservative and comfortable. (Covered calls, Ginnie Maes, Freddie Macs, collateralized mortgage obligations, assets backed by credit cards and auto loans, and real estate investment trusts all appeared speculative when first introduced, but they now are part of conventional investing. Foreign investing and managed futures are modern examples of investment concepts that are still unfamiliar to most trustees and therefore considered too speculative for most institutions.)

*   *   *   *   *

Investment committees have an unusual position in the board process. They administer. While a board routinely sets broad policy and hires the chief administrative officer, it seldom makes day-to-day decisions. In contrast, the investment committee directly retains professional advisors, authorizes payment of fees, and makes extremely important choices. With or without written authority in the charter, bylaws, or board policy statement, the investment committee's decisions usually are final. Therefore, trustees serving on the investment committee have a significant obligation, a fiduciary responsibility. Yet there also is an important connection between the board process and the investment process that is recognized when the investment committee acts with sensitivity to the needs of the organization, reports effectively to the board, coordinates with other interested constituencies, and makes decisions that produce tangible benefits. These elements of the investment committee task seem obvious, but it is not always easy to recall the larger picture when the meeting room door closes and talk turns to theoretical principals of portfolio management.

NOTES

1. Quoted in John Carver, *Boards That Make a Difference: A New Design for Leadership in Nonprofit and Public Organizations* (San Francisco: Jossey-Bass, 1991), p. 60.
2. The Atlanta Consulting Group, Inc., *Planning Inspired Performance* (Atlanta, Ga., 1988), p. 1.
3. Ibid., quoted in *Preprogram Workbook*, p. 3.
4. Ibid., quoted in *Pre Program Workbook*, p. 5.

CHAPTER 8

CREATION OF INVESTMENT GOALS

Contrary to the commonly accepted belief, it is the risk element in our capitalistic system which produces an economy of security. Risk brings out the ingenuity and resourcefulness which insure the success of enough ventures to keep the economy growing and secure.

Robert Rawls

The biggest obstacle to enterprising goal creation is the fear of risk. The solution is an investment policy that gives as much attention to risk as it does to reward.

Risk is measured by mind and by temperament, but temperament is most influential. Yesterday's burglary, for example, causes fear among the neighbors, even though there is no greater probability that the same crime will occur again today or tomorrow. Nevertheless, locks are installed, lights are lit, and crime-watch committees actually function, at least for a week or two, while efforts toward tangible improvements temporarily take a backseat. The response is to prevent recurrence of a recent event that has powerfully influenced temperament.

Throughout history, misplaced fears—"The world is flat" or "If man were intended to fly, he would have been born with wings"—have restrained human advancement. Other relevant circumstances include the following.

1. When a good friend, relative, or neighbor has a heart attack, we suddenly seek an electrocardiogram for ourselves, though the probability of our experiencing this disease has not changed.

2. Psychologists demonstrate "cognitive bias" (often a fear of the unlikely) by asking an audience, "What causes more deaths, heart disease or automobile accidents?" Usually, the show of hands favors either auto accidents or heart disease by a narrow margin, but the correct answer is heart disease, by 15 to 1.[1] The incorrect perception (misplaced fear) occurs because accidents are reported daily in the media, often with dramatic photos or videotapes, conveying an inaccurate impression through mere repetition. Hence, we are more likely to use a seat belt than to control cholesterol and to exercise.

3. Investors are susceptible to bias based only on recent trends. For example, account representatives know intuitively that investors do not want to acquire common stocks at the bottom of a bear market (following a decline in value), but it is easy for them to purchase at the top of a bull market (after a significant increase in value). The tendency is to believe that whatever happened yesterday is likely to happen again today and tomorrow. Institutions also find it easier to act when recent trends favor their point of view. An example is the 1968 Ford Foundation recommendation that endowments acquire growth securities. This advice appeared during a great bull market, when both the foundation's own policymakers and its intended audience were more likely to accept change.

Trustees face apprehensions directly by developing an investment policy, a written statement of goals that also catalogs potential risks. This is difficult because it is more interesting to imagine success than to contemplate failure. People who purchase lottery tickets must feel a powerful and pleasurable euphoria as they envision wealth and glory. If it were otherwise, they could not buy a ticket. The same is true with investors. They foresee a positive outcome, usually enhanced by the imagery of sales literature and suggestions of experienced speakers. Although technical literature does consider reward in the context of risk, few investment committees devote equal time to both. Fear of risk not only influences final decisions; it even controls meeting agendas.

It may be, however, that a thorough consideration of risk will lead to improved investment performance because the reality of risk is not as intimidating as its contemplation. In fact, risk refers to unlikely occurrences. Success is the more likely outcome in most human endeavors, except perhaps jumping from an airplane without a parachute. Therefore, the questions for trustees are simple: "What are consequences of our actions and decisions?" "How much risk can we afford?"

Just as insurance companies look at death rates to develop mortality tables, it is possible to examine historic data about securities markets to predict future volatility. Volatility is the primary indicator of risk and therefore a more important concept than loss. A focus on loss directs attention to the possible total disappearance of value at an unknown future date. As a measure of risk, loss has been part of the folklore of investing, especially in the popular advice to individuals "Never invest more than you can afford to lose!" This advice has two unfortunate components. It gives credence to an unlikely circumstance, and it dissuades investors from taking risks that probably would improve their net worth.

In reality, most portfolios have infinite lives. Even portfolios of individuals survive indefinitely as they pass from person to person through inheritance. Therefore, the most important risk of a portfolio is that it will not have sufficient value to support a future project or income need. Perhaps there will not be enough money to pay retirement plan beneficiaries when due, or to cover operating expenses of an educational institution, or to make enough grants to community service projects. This risk is a function of volatility, the possibility that a group of assets either will not appreciate to a projected level or will temporarily decline from the present value on which operating assumptions depend.

Mathematical and investment theorists have provided tools to measure past volatility. These include:

1. *Range:* the difference between recorded highs and lows.
2. *Beta:* the volatility of a stock's return relative to the market. The beta of the market always is 1.00. A security has a beta of 1.00 if it historically has changed in value at the same rate as the entire market. In other words, it typically has risen 10 percent only when the entire market also has risen 10 percent. If it consistently has moved up or down 20 percent when the market was moving up or down only 10 percent, the beta is approximately 1.09 (1.2 divided by 1.1).
3. *Standard deviation:* the measurement of the relative positions of all data contributing to computation of a mean. Roughly two thirds of all data occur within one standard deviation of the mean to which they contribute. If the standard deviation is a high number, statistics making up the mean are far apart from one another. When the standard deviation is a low number, they are closer in value. The long-term growth of a portfolio might be expressed as 9 percent, but this figure alone does not describe month-to-month or year-to-year volatility around the 9 percent mean. We cannot tell if a serious decline took place during the period. In 1987, for example, some portfolios rose 40 percent, then declined 20 percent below their January 1 values, but finished the year with 3 percent average total returns. The average gives us no hint of risks to investors who might have needed funds at the

low. If a portfolio has a standard deviation of 5 percent, two thirds of its monthly or yearly values were within 5 percent of the mean. On the other hand, a 30 percent standard deviation indicates much greater short-term volatility because many specific values were 30 percent or more above or below the mean.

Using both common language and statistical tools such as standard deviation, trustees can write their goals. They first state a specific and measurable objective, such as a 10 percent return during the next five years, and they formally agree to accept the level of risk (volatility) historically associated with that rate of return. It is important to state the risk assumption in common terms as well as in professional language so that other trustees and outside observers fully understand and appreciate both the goal and the potential consequences. If the investment goal is tied to a tangible purpose like commencing construction of a new building in five years, it becomes easy to evaluate consequences. The possibilities are obvious. First, construction might start early if returns are better than 10 percent, or it might start as scheduled, or it might start later than scheduled. Can the university tolerate this uncertainty in exchange for potentially higher returns in the long run? Trustees can answer that question, and the answer will lead them to a more precise investment policy with a higher risk tolerance and commensurate higher potential return.

(Individuals also can develop a statement of desired reward and acceptable risk. It might be expressed this way: "We want to retire at age 65 with $200,000. That will require a 14 percent annual return during the next 10 years. We know this is ambitious, and we know the risks are higher than average, but we are willing to accept the possibility of losses that might force us to retire later or to accept a lower standard of living.")

Of course, risk must be limited in some situations. An educational institution with declining enrollment, staff turmoil, and recent fire damage to two buildings probably could not afford the additional pain of a 1987-style market crash. (When it rains, it pours.) Small foundations, underfunded pension plans, and community foundations just getting started also should set low risk standards in simple language.[2] On the other hand, trustees of large pooled funds inherently have great flexibility to achieve above-average rates of return because potential declines would not force the institution to close its doors. Furthermore, if diversification is used in a variety of debt and equity markets, for a variety of tangible purposes, utilizing securities from many different companies in many different nations, it is unlikely that the entire fund will suffer major permanent losses.

WRITING POLICIES, ESTABLISHING GOALS

Effective goals, those that both unite and motivate people, have common characteristics. First, they are *specific* and have a time component. Examples are: "I want to learn to ski on intermediate slopes this year." "We will bring a personal computer to market within 24 months." "Our company will improve its return on equity to 22 percent by fiscal year XXXX." "Within the next three months, we will position ourselves to earn at least 11 percent on endowment assets."

Goals also are *measurable*. It is possible to determine in the future whether they have been achieved and to compute interim results compared to the anticipated rate of accomplishment.

Goals are *written*. An unwritten goal does not exist. Unless a decision appears as a detailed written statement, memories of its discussion and creation will fade within a week, and by the next meeting trustees will disagree as to what was decided. There should be as many words dedicated to the risk assumption as to objectives. Other trustees and investment managers cannot interpret and carry out the statement unless it clearly relates reward to risk in a consistent manner. While it makes no sense to state, "Safety of principal is our primary goal," and then to authorize purchase of such volatile assets as common stocks, it does make sense to authorize common stocks within a policy clearly accepting stock market risks.

Most goals are *aggressive*. They declare a "stretch," an attempt to reach a level of performance that will be notable, above the average. Unfortunately, most investment policies written today are trite, reflecting agreement on only the most conventional concepts. Committees are comfortable with the commonplace, fearful of the new and different. I have yet to read an investment policy drawn in the competitive language of business or athletics that states, "We want to be the best, and we are willing to assume the required risks to be the best. We want our institution to provide outstanding service with excellent facilities and well-paid staff. Our investment program must assist in this effort by realizing rates of return significantly better than those of our peers.'' But this stretch is great. While trustees acknowledge that creating a superior institution arises from assuming calculated, diversified risk, their actions gravitate to the customs of their peers. Whatever everyone else is doing is fine with them. This makes reading investment policies as exciting as donning an old T-shirt.

NOTES

1. Diseases of heart: 293.6 per 100,000 population in 1989; motor vehicle accidents: 18.9. *The World Almanac and Book of Facts, 1991,* (New York: Pharos Books, 1991), p. 836.
2. On the other hand, an underfunded pension plan has the least to lose and the most to gain from an aggressive investment program. Therefore, this assertion demonstrates the pitfalls of making an assertion.

CHAPTER 9

WHO SHOULD JOIN THE INVESTMENT COMMITTEE

All mankind is divided into three classes: Those that are immovable, those that are movable, and those that move.

Arabian proverb

At first light, children learn how to spend, and within their first decade parents teach them how to earn. But people learn investing concepts, if at all, during the years after majority, at a significant cost in intellectual sweat and practical experience. Earning and spending are tangible, naturally acquired functions, but investing is fundamentally intangible. It involves trust, comprehension of time, some knowledge of statistics, an intuitive understanding of risk, personal acceptance of the unpredictability of life's events, and a sense of excitement. This sense of excitement motivates investors to take the field, to play the game despite possible short-term injury or loss. Unlike the native knowledge of spending and earning, the intangible concepts of investing will be discovered only in the words and experiences of hundreds of professional and amateur investors who actually have played the game. New investors may *study* investing, but then they must *do* it themselves. It's like swimming—you must jump in to learn!

Because they have learned the language of administration merely by living American life, decision makers for retirement plans and foundations/endowments take their chairs with intuitive, mutual understanding of how to get an organization started (staff, bylaws, liability insurance); how to raise money (sell a product, visit philanthropists, collect retirement plan contributions); and how to budget expenditures. While some proclaim to feel discomfort while making charitable solicitations, they do understand the jargon, organizational structure, and techniques required to do it, or they can evaluate proposals by fund-raising specialists. Board members also are prepared to develop and approve a budget. They may have taken courses on how to budget, how to run a business, or how to structure family finances; or they may have achieved a working knowledge of budgeting through experience. Probably, every board member is personally comfortable debating these issues and arriving at a consensus because all trustees are familiar with the problems and the opportunities, as well as the self-evident necessity to complete revenue and spending plans.

To the degree that most board members are self-assured when discussing income and expenditures, they may be uncertain and self-conscious when considering investment issues, in part because they have limited personal experience. Their attitudes about investing may be dominated by fear of its perceived complexity or by fear of loss. On any board, only a few members—if any—will have attempted to compete in the investment marketplace, and some of those already will have experienced difficulties that have convinced them that the water is unsafe, that it is to be feared. Hence, many board members are uncomfortable with finance. They state, "I really don't understand the markets; they are too sophisticated," which may be a way of expressing apprehension and doubt, the uncertainty that fertilizes an unspoken desire to leave this task to others.

Who, then, is going to supervise the endowment or retirement plan? The answer: Anyone can do it. A punster would say that supervising investments will generate personal dividends to anyone who has the interest. But how does a board or a committee find the right people? To answer that question, let's look again at the nature of a board of directors.

It may be argued that the obligations of board members are greater than the honor, but most directors are selected as an honor, a recognition of their business or civic achievements. They also may be asked to serve on a board to maintain, or to obtain, institutional support for the organization. Certainly, large public institutions—such as community and fraternal foundations, the United Way, scout troops, art museums, and universities—invite individuals to be trustees because of their position within the community. Retirement plan trustees are named according to their position within the company or in their capacity as representative of a group of employees. Social action organizations—such as groups dealing with drug abuse or the homeless, religious organizations, health improvement societies, and education/scholarship funds—normally seek volunteer trustees who have been heavily involved with the cause over long periods. In other words, individuals become trustee/leaders because they have earned respect in the real world—not because they have earned recognized competence in investments and investment theory.

A related difficulty is that leaders in industry and finance who tend to appear on important boards of directors have spent their adult lives dealing in the corporeal world of goal setting, incentive establishment, and cost control, or they are recognized experts and leaders in social action. As a group, they tend to believe that "getting the job done" is *the* important value. They are highly focused, as shown by the kinds of goals they create: "We will raise $10 million this year!" "We will train 42 teachers of the gifted and talented, who will then start classes for 600 students by June 199X!" "We will recruit 800 freshmen this year." "We will sell 6,000 superhundred laptop computers by March." These are plain, specific, measurable, declarable goals suitable to real-world action and progress.

In their careers, these individuals know where they are going and how to get there, and many already have arrived. They feel in charge of their lives; they are competitive and motivated; they value their time; and they seek achievement wherever they serve. It is therefore ironic that these combined experiences, attitudes, and achievements may in fact produce individuals who are singularly unsuitable to manage money and distinctly intolerant of market cycles. They also may be unable to share with one another an understanding of investment principles. They may understand the definitions of *interest rate, maturity, dividend,* or *stock exchange index,* but their collective minds wander when the words *standard deviation, beta,* and *duration* hit the agenda. Then they prefer to "leave it to the experts," to delegate this important one third of their responsibility to a select committee or to investment professionals—without providing the kinds of clear instruction necessary to create appropriate investment strategies. They are generals who say "Go fight," without saying when and where. It appears true, therefore, that a thorough discussion of risk tolerance compared to potential reward seldom takes place at the board level because most directors are uncomfortable with the language and principles of this apparently vaporous craft.

Who, then, gets the job? Is it possible that leadership of investment activities is delegated to directors who have the least enthusiasm, while the most interested and qualified are given other tasks or no tasks at all? Could it be that the obvious choice is wrong and that the most thorough work will be pursued by individuals who appear to be least qualified and interested? Could it be that finding interested and effective leadership is similar to locating investment assets selling at bargain prices, a difficult task that must be pursued relentlessly by searching in obscure places? It is a fact of life that we appreciate a good investment—and a successful investor—only by hindsight.

During the organization phase, new boards assign tasks to individuals according to how they are perceived professionally. The attorney will be assigned to write bylaws, to file with the secretary of state, and to act as legal counsel. An accountant will be named treasurer. The board elects as president/chairperson the one who pushed to create the organization in the first place, while investment management is given to individuals who work for financial services companies, such as life insurance, banking, investment banking, trust, or stock brokerage. These appointments are routine, widely accepted, and often inefficient.

Appointments by professional image are inefficient in at least two ways. The first is that many people prefer to do "something else" when they enter volunteer service, like the stock broker who said of the television show "Wall Street Week," "It must be good, but it is not for me because when I get home on Friday night I want to do something else!" If a person spends 50 or 60 hours a week pursuing excellence in law, accounting, administration, or investments, a hidden part of his or her soul continuously whispers, "Listen, you will be healthier, happier, and more complete if you leave professional obligations at the office." Neverthe less, these people accept volunteer responsibilities because it seems the right thing to do, and everyone around them says, "You definitely will do a good job in this position."

The second inefficiency is that perceived talents may not be real; an individual's credentials, business title, or position may imply experiences different from his or her actual experiences. The lawyer asked to write bylaws, for example, might be a specialist in criminal law, and the accountant asked to be treasurer could be a management consultant, and the banker selected to the investment committee may have spent his or her entire life as a branch manager and loan officer, not a professional investor in stocks and bonds. An example of this conundrum recently was mentioned by a brokerage firm account executive who had made a presentation to the investment committee of a foundation. The committee chair was executive vice president of a bank, a title causing the account executive to presume competence in investment markets. "I was talking about bonds," said the account executive, "when the chairman asked,

'Shouldn't we purchase tax-exempt securities [for the foundation]?' ''
The chairman did not understand that only taxable investors should acquire tax-exempt bonds. Foundations do not need tax-exempt income because they do not pay taxes. Clearly, this chairman was appointed
because of his reputation, not his knowledge and experience with
investing.

Large institutions, such as colleges and universities, as well as
foundations and endowments, often appoint financial services executives
to investment committees, assuming that they are inherently qualified or
at least able to draw on the resources of their organizations to accomplish
assigned tasks. It is important to note, however, that the skills of these
persons are not investment skills. Generally, they have people skills instead. They are good administrators, good public speakers, and effective
spokespersons for their companies. They know how to appoint competent
subordinates, delegate tasks, manage large transactions, and deal with
personnel, but few are schooled in the basics of impersonal investment
theories and practices. Most, in fact, prefer to delegate investment authority, because instead of investing, they administer. They deal with
people, not with investment theories and security selection.

So, who should supervise the money? Answer: Those who want to!
The desire to complete a task and personal enthusiasm for an activity are
the most important progenitors of success. An athletic director asked
why one team wins will say, "Because they want to. Their players want
to play, and they want to win. They enjoy the physical effort, the strategy, the moments of drama and excitement. They are totally involved
with the game. They love what they do and want to improve every day."

Mozart, of course, wanted to write music; Dustin Hoffman, to act;
Ray Kroc, to sell hamburgers; Peter Lynch, to invest; and Columbus, to
discover. But Columbus should be our hero, for discovery is the most exciting and stimulating reward from investing, perhaps as important as
financial gain. The individual who will produce superior results is the
one who wants to invest; who is excited by the prospect of learning about
the magical interaction between risk and reward and the essential qual-
ities of good business managers, as well as of good money managers; and
who enjoys learning a new discipline, reading about successful investors,
and talking with some of the most talented people in our nation. He
or she will take time and make extra efforts to lead the neverending task
of placing investments in a portfolio according to the risk tolerance of
its owners.

For a society in which an actor or rail splitter can be president, a classically trained Shakespearean actress can become a country humorist, and a stern-wheeler captain a great novelist. (Ronald Reagan and Abraham Lincoln, Minnie Pearl, Samuel Clemens) it becomes important to look for talent in the least likely places, to search for those individuals who will be outstanding stewards of institutional money—our money—because they love the game and want to win.

A first step is to determine who is suitable for investment responsibilities. Instead of assigning jobs, the chairperson could say, "George, I am calling to make sure that our board members are interested in assigned tasks. On this board, there is no preconceived functional obligation for a board member, but each has a duty to present his vision and to express his opinions about programs and policies. We want you to do what you like to do. Therefore, instead of arbitrarily assigning you to a committee, I want to ask what you would most like to do. Just give me an idea of what you are most qualified to do, or suggest new activities you would find interesting and challenging. I'm especially interested in filling positions on the investment committee, but we expect trustees on that committee to spend several hours each month learning about investment theory. What do you think?"

This is the direct approach, the shortest route to any destination, but it assumes that the board is being organized for the first time, that trustees do not already have self-images governing their assignments, attitudes, and actions. To the extent that a group of trustees already is organized and functions have been assigned, reorganizing may be necessary because few boards operate investment programs at peak efficiency. Most boards spend less time on their investment portfolios than on raising money and managing programs because investment subcommittees tend to make final decisions. It is rare for the full board of a nonprofit to hear presentations by money managers and consultants. Instead, subcommittee chairpersons periodically report rates of return and the names of managers hired. This means that investment committees hold unique authority. While most board committees and task forces create recommendations that require formal motions and debate, investment committees just report. They say, "We hired Modern Money Management for a short duration bond program, dismissed Eighteen Twelve Advisors for below-average performance, but still earned 9.22 percent on invested assets." That's it. A done deal. Although this arrangement has many advantages, it also has at least three deficiencies. The first deficiency is theoretical. It is that boards, not committees, should establish policy. The second is that board leadership is less sensitive to the dynamics of the investment committee and therefore less likely to appoint interested new trustees at opportune moments. Finally, boards fail to evaluate investment results relative to both their larger purposes and to results earned by other institutions.

To reorganize, a board must locate one individual willing to facilitate change, to push the board toward new ends. This person is a consultant, paid or volunteer, who understands the language of investing and the concepts of risk and reward. (As used here, *consultant* means "facilitator," the "point person" who gets things done. In other parts of this book, *consultant* means an outside advisor whose profession is to consult about investment policy and performance.) It makes no difference whether this individual receives compensation. Many effective consultants work as volunteers or as part of the professional staff, but it is impossible to manage investments without them, just as it is impossible to manage an organization without a chief executive. Private investors either act as their own consultants or work with a broker, financial planner, or investment advisor. Married couples have a consultant: the spouse who makes things happen by calling to place buy-and-sell orders. Small retirement plans have a consultant: the company officer and/or clerical assistant who calls meetings, takes notes, talks to the accountant and actuary, advises participants, and places funds in appropriate investments. Foundations/endowments have a consultant: perhaps the treasurer who organizes and executes policies.

The ideal facilitator/consultant is knowledgeable, professional, personable, generous, civic minded, impartial, and unbiased. He or she is recognized as an expert, lives in the local community, donates time, has no conflicts of interest, will not seek fee or commission income from consultative activities, believes in the cause, is trusted by every other board member, has good rapport with both the staff and the board chairman, and consistently has earned 18 percent per year on his or her personal investment portfolio without a single down year. He also flies without wings and walks on water. Considering the difficulty of finding this expert, a board might have to accept someone of lesser talents who will arrive at board meetings by automobile, occasionally bearing a burden of slight mistrust.

In a culture that suspects conflict of interest to the same degree it praises achievement, mistrust will be a subtle force in determining who administers the fund. If the consultant/facilitator is a professional investor, working either for compensation or as a volunteer, the board will have to measure his or her skills and credibility within a slight fog of suspicion. Only senators and members of congress, the "self-serving politicians," are subject to more criticism and suspicion than financial experts. Just as taverns are filled with patrons griping about politicians, boardroom hallways feature a few who think that investment experts seek only a fee or commission. Every consultant, paid or volunteer, works in this milieu of questioned motivations and challenged ethics. It is part of the territory, endemic to the job, because people believe that the fee and commission system is biased. Also, the result of any advisor's recommendation or action is known within a short period because investment accounts compute values daily. No other business is measured so quickly, so precisely.

Yet effective boards and committees do confer trust by acknowledging the unique position of the consultant/facilitator. It confidently allows him or her to direct meetings toward a consensus expressed in policies that reflect the board's view of itself. These statements should appear in the minutes and should definitively describe the acceptable level of risk; the restrictions, if any, on investment activities; and the percentage of assets it wants to spend each year.

Conferring trust is a conscious act, sometimes explicitly expressed. It is a message that the group both appreciates and comprehends what the consultant must try to do. That is, the consultant does not determine policy or even strongly advocate a specific policy. Instead, he or she directs discussion impartially to focus attention on important matters, to help it govern by expressing its decisions in language that is distinct and understandable to someone who is not on the board and who did not participate in the debate. The consultant helps the board avoid meaningless deliberations about details such as maturities, the choice of custodian, accounting principles, and the thousand other topics boards debate while failing to make policy. The consultant writes decisions in professional language, avoiding publication of restrictions not intended by the board, while precisely describing the risks it has agreed to assume. Next, the board transcribes its policies in the minutes and keeps records of its deliberations in a separate file. (Usually, only the minutes survive long periods.) This assures that future trustees can research original intent, for policies not written soon are policies forgotten.

When a board, an entire board, has adopted investment goals and policies appropriate to its vision, it then seeks trustees genuinely interested in supervising implementation. This is difficult. Trustees do not

---

TABLE 9-1
Decision-Making Models

The Classic Model

Board chairperson appoints investment committee
↓
Investment committee writes all policies
↓
Investment committee hires consultants and managers
↓
Investment committee monitors results and reports to board

An Alternative Model

With assistance of consultant/facilitator entire board (or corporate executive committee) creates investment and spending policies
↓
Board leadership searches for investment committee trustees (who want to carry out the policy)
↓
Investment committee examines policies, proposes amendments, sets goals, writes restrictions, reports long-term effects of board's spending policy
↓
Full board ratifies policies
↓
Investment committee implements

---

easily or candidly disclose personal feelings about proposed responsibilities, and some boards will find no one with genuine intuitive enthusiasm for the investment process.

The most important characteristic of an effective investment committee member is personal commitment, a singular enthusiasm about achieving notable results. This enthusiasm will appear as intense curiosity about securities markets, because the desire to learn is a more powerful motivator than experience. Furthermore, boards seldom have enough ''experienced investors'' to fill a committee roster.

The second most important personal characteristic of a potentially effective trustee/supervisor is flexibility, represented by willingness to listen and to learn new ideas. Since superior returns may be achieved by those who carry out new ideas—before the ideas become conventional wisdom—investment committee trustees need to be free of preconceived notions that one approach is speculative or another conservative. A new idea might appear speculative merely because it is new, and investment accounts that wait until an idea or strategy is widely accepted will achieve only average results by using it. An example is asset-backed securities, which sold at low prices when first introduced. Use of listed options as an investment hedge is a conservative method to protect value, but it appeared speculative when introduced. Trading futures is an innovation that might prove useful, but boards give it little attention. The reason is that most investors believe futures trading is speculating in commodities prices. (Managed futures may turn out to be inappropriate for most institutions, but boards should study it.)

Time is a third asset of a conscientious trustee of investment. To serve well, to develop a broad sense of risk and reward, an individual must apportion personal time, usually in creative ways. He or she must be willing to talk frequently with brokers, advisors, trust investment officers, the organization's own professional staff, and its professional money managers, as well as other investors and other trustees in similar positions. Willingness to ask powerful questions is important. A question like "What do you think the market will do this year?" elicits predictions but not information. On the other hand, "How do automotive stocks correlate with oil stocks in a portfolio?" and "Tell me all you know about CMOs" are open-ended queries that lead to meaningful discussion and new insights about how markets work. Trustees need to create opportunities to ask questions by attending meetings of financial analysts, seminars about modern investment techniques, and after-hour social encounters with professional money managers. To do all this, a trustee responsible for investments needs time.

The commitment of time includes a commitment to read. Investment-related literature is voluminous but fun to read. A committed trustee who spends three to five hours a week could read most of the items in this book's bibliography within a year and through that effort would review over 100 years of investment experience. Any person unwilling to do this should not be appointed regardless of title, position, or perceived experience. But a trustee who pledges to read should be appointed immediately even if he or she is 23 years old, wears sweaters, makes $23,000 per year, and appears self-conscious.

While a board will be lucky to find curiosity, flexibility, time, and willingness to read all packaged neatly in one individual, our superman/trustee also should have a capacity to see the essence of any matter. He or she should have a predisposition to lead and to present potentially unpopular points of view, as well as a facility to delegate, to achieve results through others.

The least important criterion is experience, especially in the trustee who views his or her investment experiences with remorse. There is nothing worse than a portfolio supervised by individuals and groups of individuals who have had negative investment experiences, are pessimistic and cynical, and are unlikely to place their trust with conviction and loyalty. Boards should remove these persons from investment activities because they criticize, see risk without potential reward, push for frequent changes of money management personnel, and make everyone miserable. They cause organizations to miss opportunities.

An informal consensus among those who professionally serve both retirement plan and nonprofit investment committees is that a board (or company officers, in the case of a retirement plan) makes policy when it names members of the investment committee because those individuals bring to the table both skills and baggage that predetermine or at least significantly influence decisions. This is why policy should precede people and why trustees appointed to the investment committee should support policy. This is to say *who* is as important as *what*.

See Appendix 3 for a job description and questionnaire regarding the characteristics of an effective, interested trustee.

CHAPTER 10

WRITING AN INVESTMENT POLICY STATEMENT

The chief merit of language is clearness, and we know that nothing detracts so much from this as do unfamiliar terms.

Galen

Investment policies must be simple, forthright, and understandable to a competent stranger.[1] They declare a goal, accept risk, and enumerate prohibited transactions. That's all. Nothing more. It can be done in a page and a half.

Investment policies represent the most important statement of committee consensus, but they fail an important test: No one reads them. They are imprecise, impersonal, and only marginally effective. And they are dull. The path to improvement starts with expressions of organizational and committee vision, followed by risk assumptions, allocation of assets, and criteria for manager retention—all in common language that is understandable to a competent stranger as well as to the organization's supporters and beneficiaries.

Most policies confuse even their authors. The following is an example of a virtually incomprehensible policy statement:

> We recognize eternal tension between the high demand for immediate income and the enduring need for a growing stream of future income to meet future needs. Therefore, our fund should be managed on a pool basis that includes debt and equity securities. We will meet the goal of current income and asset growth through the fund asset mix policy. All income from funds invested in debt securities will be distributed, but income from equity securities will be distributed according to a spending policy established from time to time by this committee. We will maintain an asset mix policy expressed in terms of policy weights to be reviewed once a year. We will compare our returns to returns on the passively implemented policy asset mix estimated by calculating the rate of return on an appropriately weighted blend of designated asset classes. Our need for future income shall not be sacrificed for the immediate need. Our bias is toward

equity securities, subject only to liquidity requirements and limitations on volatility.

This hodgepodge of literary vacuity emerged from numerous meetings over two years. It is incomprehensible to a professional investment manager (the competent stranger who must carry out its instructions), because it states only that the committee will create specific policies. It does not say what the committee believes right now. Hence, a money manager or consultant cannot determine from this document whether its proprietary techniques and philosophies are appropriate for this institution. In addition, words such as *bias* and *passively implemented policy mix* communicate indecision, not firm direction.

The following is another example:

> Foundation funds will be invested with emphasis on long-term growth of total market value. The investment managers shall be guided by the Prudent Man rule. The equity and fixed income portions shall be reviewed separately, even if a balanced manager is selected, and compared to the equity market index such as the S&P 500 and the fixed income market index such as the Shearson Lehman Aggregate, respectively. Performance will be monitored on a rolling 3-year basis. The selected indexes should be consistent with thoughts about equity yield, fixed income maturity, etc. and also with the style of the selected investment managers. We should use straightforward, broad, well-diversified strategies with favorable risk-reward characteristics. It is the responsibility of the investment committee to manage the allocation of assets among equity, debt and other investments. As a general rule, no more than 35 percent of the Fund shall be in fixed income instruments and no more than 65 percent of the Fund shall be invested in equities including convertibles.

This is useless "committee speak." Even allowing that private correspondence might provide more guidance, the policy establishes vague standards without criteria either for purchasing securities or measuring results. It creates more questions than answers. Does the committee expect results to be better than the S&P 500? If it is satisfied with results of that index itself, should it acquire a fund that duplicates the index? Will they fire an investment manager if his or her results are less than average? What are "favorable risk-reward characteristics"? In the eyes of this account, what is the definition of a prudent man? (See the glossary for one definition.) Does "fixed income" mean bonds, or does it include preferreds with fixed dividends? What is a "straightforward, broad, well-diversified''strategy? The 35/65 percent limitation is unworkable. If the committee later elects 50 percent equities, and is restricted by policy to 35 percent fixed income, then 15 percent may not be invested in anything at all. Before mandating straightforward strategies, this committee should write in straightforward language.

To explain in more detail, the policy "65 percent equity, 35 percent fixed income" poses problems. This committee probably believes that its asset allocation *always* will be about 65 percent equities, 35 percent fixed income, but instead of mandating this allocation, the sentence beginning "As a general rule, no more than" is indecisive. The committee assumes that money not invested in either category will be invested in a third asset class, cash equivalents, that often is ignored in written investment policies. Committees fail to mention cash for two reasons: (1) They implicitly predict that managers always will be fully invested, and (2) cash does not appear to be an asset class requiring committee attention. But if we consider only issues of clarity and governance, the committee should have been more thorough and direct. How would the committee feel if the bond and stock managers both withdrew 50 percent from their respective markets? That would leave almost half the total account in cash. Is that OK? Perhaps. We do not know. Some committees do want 65 percent in the stock market at all times, but they also want their managers to have flexibility. This is achieved by temporarily purchasing a stock market index fund with cash generated by a manager.

Let's look at one more example, with comments in brackets:

> The overriding *investment objective* is to follow those policies that will protect the principal value of the endowment and provide predictable income. [*Principal* cannot be understood without adjectives. One dictionary suggests that it refers to a sum of money or a total value on a certain date, as in "the principal of our endowment is $100 million." In this sense, the phrase *protect principal* prohibits a meaningful decline in value from the starting date. Principal also is the stated value, or "face value," of a bond or certificate at maturity. In strict usage, the only way to protect principal is to acquire securities that change little in price from day to day, or to maintain a portfolio of bonds having a calculable principal. *Principal* also is an accounting term that distinguishes original capital from income earned on that capital.] Because a substantial part of our spendable income is the result of earnings on endowment, endowment management is more income-oriented than would be the case in most other academic institutions. [Apparently, the committee has surveyed other institutions and

believes it is important to cite this difference. However, the importance of the difference is obscure because it is not quantified.] At the same time, protection against inflation is not to be neglected, so at least 50 percent of endowment is to be invested in common stock with a history of dividend growth and good prospects. [Now it seems the investment manager may buy equity securities, a category inherently having no principal to protect. This anomaly appears in numerous investment policies because most investment committees subliminally want to have their cake and eat it, too. Nevertheless, it is impossible both to protect principal and to invest in marketable securities such as stocks and bonds.] This general guideline is not intended to preclude the purchase of selected low yielding common stocks with unusual growth potentials. [Does this mean companies with small capitalizations and high betas and standard deviations? The historic volatility of this sector is very high. Is this committee ready to accept the declining portion of volatile cycles? Does such a decline conflict with the goal of protecting principal value? Who can tell? The competent stranger observes only mutually exclusive mandates and suggestions. He or she does not know what to do.]

Because they are drawn randomly from the work of small nonprofit institutions managed by volunteers, these three statements do not represent the thousands of existent investment policies. There are many well-written policies, especially for retirement plans run by full-time professionals. Meanwhile, professional journals frequently present excellent prototype policies.[2] Yet our examples do illustrate that some policies are worse than no policy. Clarity of language and precise use of words are crucial to investment success because the policy must be understood by four important collaborating teams. These are the current investment committee and board of trustees, the investment managers who carry out policy, supporters of the organization such as alumni or retirement plan beneficiaries, and future trustees who want to understand why specific decisions were made in the past.

Clear, useful, effective investment policies arise from the synthesis of *governance* and *portfolio* theories. Governance theory proposes managing ends instead of means. In the words of John Carver,

> Strategic leadership is proclaimed more through wisely developed organizational ends than through any other aspect of governance. This policy category could be called results, impacts, goals, or outcomes as well as ends, each title having its connotations. . . . The only justifiable reason for organizational existence is the production of worthwhile results. . . . Lead-

ership for results begins outside, not inside the organization. . . . The most effective way to help a board rise above organizational myopia is to let the board taste the grand expanse of the larger context.[3]

Therefore, the first sentences of an investment policy should remind readers that the real purpose is not to invest but rather to serve people, to satisfy social, educational, or retirement needs. Next, the investment committee should describe its role in achieving the goals of the organization. It should define its own purposes in writing, specifically stating what it expects to do to facilitate real-life accomplishments. Then the following advice applies:

> Investment managers and clients [should] agree objectively on each of these important policy dimensions:
>
> 1. The level of market risk to be taken.
> 2. Whether the level of risk is to be sustained or varied as markets change.
> 3. Whether individual stock risk or group risk are to be taken or avoided, and the incremental rate of return which such risks, when taken, are expected to produce in the portfolio.[4]

The important final step is a clarity test, effectively executed only by strangers. The draft should be reviewed for intelligibility by individuals who had nothing to do with writing it, such as spouses, secretaries, alumni or beneficiaries, and one or two professional investors, who need to answer only two questions: "Do you understand what this says?" and "Assuming you were our investment manager, does it give you enough information and instructions to build a portfolio?" Respondents should not be allowed to give the safe, diplomatic, it-sure-looks-fine-to-me response. Instead, they must tell it like it is, for it is rare that direct criticism does not bring about considerable rewriting and substantial improvement in the committee's most important document.

HYPOTHETICAL INVESTMENT POLICIES

Because action must follow theory, two investment policies are presented below. They are extreme and would not be appropriate for most institutions. They attempt to show that plan sponsors can give useful directions to a competent stranger by describing the institution's unique character and purposes, as well as by stating goals and risk assumptions.

TABLE 10–1
Asset Allocation Summary (Probable Range of Annualized Returns within 1 Standard Deviation*)

Allocation by Percentages	Low	Expected	High	Probability of a Loss Once Every "X" Years
100 Equities	−9.5	11.5	32.5	3.5
80 Equities/20 Bonds	−6.6	10.6	27.8	3.8
80 Equities/10 Bonds/10 Cash	−6.5	10.5	27.5	3.8
80 Equities/20 Cash	−6.4	10.4	27.2	3.8
60 Equities/40 Bonds	−3.8	9.6	23.0	4.3
60 Equities/20 Bonds/20 Cash	−3.5	9.5	22.5	4.3
60 Equities/40 Cash	−3.3	9.3	21.9	4.5
40 Equities/60 Bonds	−1.2	8.7	18.6	6.3
40 Equities/30 Bonds/30 Cash	−0.7	8.4	17.5	5.9
40 Equities/60 Cash	−0.2	8.2	16.6	6.3
20 Equities/80 Bonds	0.8	7.7	14.6	8.3
20 Equities/40 Bonds/40 Cash	2.1	7.4	12.7	14.3
20 Equities/80 Cash	2.8	7.1	11.4	16.7
100 Bonds	1.3	6.8	12.3	10.0
100 Cash	5	6.0	7.0	Remote

*By definition, (1) standard deviation would indicate a 66% probability that an event will occur. In this case, the investor has a 66% probability that an annual return will fall somewhere between the ranges indicated.

Courtesy, SEI Wealth Management Services, Inc., 1990.

This table and table 10–2 show probable results from different asset allocation strategies that emerge from investment policies. Note the counterintuitive prediction that 20 percent equities/80 percent cash has less risk than 100 percent bonds.

TABLE 10-2
The "Real" Return (Percentage Invested in Stocks/Bonds)

	0% Stocks 100% Bonds	30% Stocks 70% Bonds	50% Stocks 50% Bonds	70% Stocks 30% Bonds	100% Stocks 0% Bonds
Expected income yield	8.0%	6.5%	5.5%	4.5%	3.0%
Expected long-term total return (income *plus* capital appreciation)	8.0%	9.2%	10.0%	10.8%	12.0%
Less: expected inflation	5.0%	5.0%	5.0%	5.0%	5.0%
Equals: expected real return	3.0%	4.2%	5.0%	5.8%	7.0%
Less: investment-related fees	1.5%	1.5%	1.5%	1.5%	1.5%
Less: spending policy	5.0%	5.0%	5.0%	5.0%	5.0%
Equals: Net change in real principal value	(3.5%)	(2.3%)	(1.5%)	(0.7%)	0.5%

Average
endowment foundation

By including inflation, investment-related fees, and spending policy, this table predicts that only a 100 percent allocation to stocks will produce a "real" increase in purchasing power.

The first policy is for the imaginary Safety in Aviation Foundation, which was created by three families, each having two members on the board. The families gave a total of $3 million. It is an especially personal institution formed after tragedy. As such, it does not have the fiduciary obligations to retirees as qualified retirement plans do; the commitment to civic beneficiaries, as community foundations do; or the commitment to future students, as college endowments do. Unlike most investment pools, it may take unusual risks.

Investment Policy of the Safety in Aviation Foundation

The mission of the Safety in Aviation Foundation is to reduce aviation accidents. We will do this by funding projects that study effects of ice on air foils, improve methods to both predict and communicate icing conditions, and create new technologies to remove ice in flight. We want to do this rapidly because each board member lost a relative in an ice-related accident. We are willing to take significant investment risks to achieve our goals.[5]

Our managers should facilitate cash distributions of $250,000 each year for 10 years. This money will go to research. The second goal is to double endowment value within 10 years. (Hence, the required internal rate of return is 13.6 percent on a starting value of $3 million.) In addition, we want investment assets that can be liquidated quickly should we discover additional projects. We will take risks commensurate with high investment returns, including the risk of temporary declines in market value. We can take higher risks because (1) we pay projected research costs in advance (there is little danger a project will not be completed for lack of funds); (2) we can achieve our goal within 10 years; (3) no person depends solely on us for personal financial health and retirement comfort; (3) the result (safe flying) is important compared to risk of failure, for the unlikely decline or demise of our endowment would cause minor injury, but our success will save many lives.

Our investment managers will pursue superior returns. This means a heavy concentration in small capitalization stocks. We do not seek risk reduction through diversification or balance. Instead, we seek the best possible returns. Our managers may look to four market segments. These are (1) large American companies ("blue chips" or "large caps") selling at unusually low prices (low price-earnings ratios compared to the market or to a company's historic average PE); new and emerging companies ("small caps"); (3) companies from other countries whose economies will grow;

and (4) new investment concepts that appear to have value precisely because they are new. We want to maintain these risks through strong and weak markets, and we expect substantial volatility.

The second policy is for a college in difficulty. It needs stable investments because a major (albeit temporary) decline in endowment market value could spell its permanent demise.

Investment Policy for a College in Difficulty

We are recovering from hard times. We have 500 fewer students than five years ago and reduced revenues, but expenses increased following the fire that destroyed Old East Main, our largest building. The board of trustees and the investment committee agree that our institutional existence would be threatened if the endowment value declines. Therefore, our investment manager will maintain value by acquiring only Treasury securities to produce a portfolio average life of nine months or less. There shall be no variation from this policy.

Meanwhile, we are working to expand financial resources through fundraising, student recruitment, and the positive attitude for which our institution is known. We expect our efforts to give us the financial flexibility to assume greater investment risks in about three years.

These two policies are personal. Both express unique circumstances and real-world goals, as well as candor. They convey purpose, exhibit an appealing frankness about what trustees believe and want to accomplish, and avoid expressions like "passively implemented policy asset mix" or "more income-oriented than other institutions." Ideally, an investment policy is easy to read and attractively expressed so that upon reading it an outsider wants to support the organization.

EMPLOYEE BENEFIT PLANS

Most investment policies are for employee benefit plans. It is difficult to write them well, to make them both effective and readable, because meaningless terms go from mind to typewriter faster than political promises. It is much too easy to write such things as "beat the XX index" over a "rolling three-year period" to produce "respectable" returns with "low volatility" while seeking "constancy and smoothness of value" in

---

TABLE 10–3
Elements of an Investment Policy Statement

Of the many purposes of investment policy, the most important is to communicate instructions. The policy tells managers how to manage.

1. What is the important end, or goal, of our investment program? What is to be achieved in the real world of projects, programs, and possibilities? What is the *purpose* to be enhanced by the investment program?

2. How does the board feel about its responsibilities? What are its philosophies? What is its *vision?*

3. In ordinary language, how much *risk* can the organization tolerate? What magnitude of decline would cause irreparable damage to tangible purposes? (It is not possible to predict or to assure appreciation, but it is possible to avoid most forms of loss.)

4. What is the *attitude* toward investment managers? What specific circumstances would prompt dismissal?

5. Should risk be maintained at all times? Does the investment manager have responsibility to *time,* to purchase or sell depending on his or her prediction of future price trends? Should the manager sell securities and go to cash if he or she believes that a market segment has appreciated unreasonably?

6. May the manager assume *narrow risks,* such as concentrating in a few stocks or in only a few groups of stocks? Or, must the manager diversify to assume only risks of the market as a whole?

7. Are any investments *unacceptable* (e.g., below-investment-grade bonds, securities of competing firms, companies in socially unacceptable businesses)?

8. Is our policy *understandable* and *practical?* Do beneficiaries and observers understand the intent? Do investment managers believe it is a practical policy without internal inconsistencies? Can any trustee, participant, or observer articulate the policy in three minutes or less?

"traditional" American companies. (In the first draft of this chapter, I included a hypothetical retirement plan policy that prompted this response from a critic: "You are guilty of the same sins of generalization [that you propose to eliminate]. You include vague, undefined words that are just fluff." And I thought, It is so much easier to advise than to do.)

Society has a vested interest in the financial health of its older, retired citizens; law, regulation, and custom call for written policies that protect retirement plans and their beneficiaries, thereby reducing a potential taxpayer obligation to pay welfare expenses or guarantees to retirement plans in default. Hence, retirement plan trustees should dedicate as many hours as necessary to develop a comprehensive investment policy that complies with all legal requirements, and retirement plan investment committees should evaluate their governance to be sure it facilitates and encourages continuous debate and review. In addition to communicating legal and ethical standards, the policy should outline those aspects that make a plan unique. This helps investment managers to abide by the committee's philosophies, and it reduces expensive, painful changes of managers.

The following language is for the sections of a hypothetical retirement plan investment policy that speak to goals and philosophies:

> We are employees[6] of Hardmicro Corporation, manufacturers of plastic parts for personal computers. Our company was founded in 1985 and has experienced spectacular growth. To the extent we have benefited from technological innovation, we know also that innovation by others and normal business competition could damage our business if we don't create new products and services. We believe that creativity and innovation take place in workplaces that have a minimum of personal distractions such as apprehension about future personal economic security. It follows that we have instituted a defined benefit plan to provide a predictable standard of living. Our job is to assure that predicted benefits are available when due.

The policy also should explain minimum returns stated by the actuary, limits on projected volatility, and other restrictions. It should allocate assets and specifically define responsibilities of investment managers. Written criteria for retaining managers assure both continuity and manager loyalty because every person works more effectively under an umbrella of clear expectations. The committee should send its policy draft to an attorney, and it should circulate the final draft among a select group of beneficiaries who will answer these questions: Is it clear? Is it reasonable? Does it express your feelings about your plan?

SPENDING POLICY

The last act in the policy play is to spend. Spending by retirement plans is payment of benefits prescribed in plan documents. Nonprofit spending is a different matter; trustees should deal with it in policy documents. It is more a problem of governance than of language because the main question is, Who decides how much to spend? Invariably, trustees on the investment committee want to spend less. That helps to preserve value, to increase total rates of return, and to beat inflation by compounding dividends and interest. But trustees on the finance committee want endowment support to pay salaries and to build new buildings.

Some comments at a recent conference of endowment and foundation executives summarized the spending challenge. One person said, "Trustees lust to spend 5 percent," a common rate. Another said, "Almost everyone wants to protect against inflation, but many spending policies do not allow this to happen." Another person asked, "How much can we tell the faculty [about endowment value and spending] without them getting too greedy?" And this observation: "Retrospection reigns [in the design of spending policies]! Spending policies based on historical investment returns might not work. Things have been going too well. I've seen the 21st century—and it's not the 1980s. The common wisdom will be tested."

Policy statements handle any spending rate in two or three sentences, but the question remains, who decides? A suggestion is to create a special committee, hopefully one that meets infrequently. Members would be representatives of the nonprofit's professional staff, finance and investment committees, and other affected constituencies. The committee decides how much to spend. Therefore, it decides whether to emphasize current needs by spending now or to save for future needs by preserving assets.

* * * * *

What makes a good investment policy? Charles Ellis proposes these simple tests:

1. Is the policy carefully designed to meet the real needs and objectives of this specific client?
2. Is the policy written so clearly and explicitly that a *competent stranger* could manage the portfolio and conform to the client's intention?
3. Would the client have been able to sustain commitment to the policies during the capital markets that have actually been experienced over the past 50 or 60 years—particularly over the past 10 years?
4. Would the investment manager have been able to maintain fidelity to the policy over the same periods?
5. Would the policy, if implemented, have achieved the client's objectives?

Sound investment policies will meet *all* of these tests. Do yours?[7]

ANOTHER TALE OF TWO POLICIES

This chapter contains excerpts from several investment policies, but which are strong and which are weak? A professional critic suggested that one of the policies described in this chapter as good is in fact weak and that another policy described as weak is in fact effective. He proposed that the policy criticized should be praised, while the other should be more thoroughly scrutinized. We exchanged written views over more than eight weeks without fully resolving our conflicting perspectives. But there is a lesson, for in this exercise the critic and I demonstrated exactly what happens in an investment committee. Investment committees seldom take enough time on their most important task—preparation of goals and policies—to satisfy every committee member. Inevitably, some members are left out, their views cast aside and ignored, not out of disrespect, but because it is so difficult to write a policy that is acceptable, readable, and effective.

Most of the above-mentioned differences between the critic and I concerned subtle meanings, technical interpretations, and idea placement in the policy or some other document. Examples are:

- "Prudent man" (the divergence between its theoretical meaning and application).
- Measuring results (comparing to a published index or to an organization's real needs).
- Should a policy list asset classes implied by the words *fixed Income?*
- Does a good policy directly authorize cash as an asset class, or is it understood to be acceptable by implication and necessity?
- What does a committee mean when it says "protect principal"?
- Are words such as *superior returns, unusually low prices,* and *unusual risks* vague or precise?
- Should a committee declare a time frame for accepting risks?
- Should personal observations about the nature of an organization appear in the written policy, in other documents such as an employee benefits handbook, or in both?

The critic and I don't have to agree on language because we are not interested in policy per se. Our work is theoretical; we are not managing an account. Also, there are many fine examples of policies in other texts, and I am sure that with enough labor he and I could have arrived at agreement. The task of this book is not to present the ideal policy, but to analyze how organizations create policy. We are examining governance.

If the colonies could agree on the Declaration of Independence and the Constitution, then investment committees can agree on policy, but it takes a lot of effort. The process is excruciating for the leader who pushes for consensus against a wall built of divergent perspectives and even boredom. Members silently ask, "Is this really worth it?" As John Maynard Keynes once observed,

---

ANOTHER TALE OF TWO POLICIES: (*continued*)

The game of professional investment is intolerably boring and overexacting to anyone who is entirely exempt from the gambling instinct; whilst he who has it must pay to this propensity the appropriate toll.[8]

But if a policy is circulated among all members, with plenty of time for written comment and an open spirit that any opinion is OK, the job will be done. And, if the task is pursued by someone who can write, or if the product is given for review to a person schooled in the potential elegance of language, an important *and* interesting document just might emerge.

(*concluded*)

NOTES

1. *Competent stranger* means a qualified person who is not personally familiar with an investment account. The concept is important because portfolio managers making day-to-day investment decisions might not be the same individuals who meet with the account.
2. Professionals occasionally confuse both themselves and their clients by debating meaningless issues such as whether goals and restrictions should appear in a policy, a strategy statement, or in manager guidelines.
3. John Carver, *Boards That Make a Difference,* (San Francisco: Jossey-Bass, 1991), pp. 35, 56, 57.
4. Charles D. Ellis, *Investment Policy,* (Homewood, Ill.: Business One Irwin, 1985), ICFA edition, p. 58.
5. Most policies do not include personal statements, but this one explains *why* the manager may take greater-than-normal risks.
6. Usually, trustees are employees, but some investment committees include individuals who are not employees.
7. Ibid., p. 62.
8. Quoted in Adam Smith, *The Money Game* (New York: Random House, 1968), p. 9.

CHAPTER 11

INVESTMENT THEORIES AND PRACTICE

The theory of probabilities is at bottom nothing more than common sense reduced to calculus.

Pierre Simon de Laplace

Theory helps us bear our ignorance of fact.

George Santayana

The battles for trustee attention pit a small platoon of ideas against a full army of aspirations and wishful thinking. The platoon wages war with self-evident truths, such as "No one can predict the future"; "Investing is an art, not a science"; "Patience and persistence produce profit"; "Diversification is useful and quantifiable"; and "What happened yesterday might not happen tomorrow." We acknowledge these truths and respect their utility, but part of us still wants to believe that we can predict with accuracy that tomorrow's events will be like yesterday's. The army of hope fights for recognition at that peculiar place where decisions are based on longing for order, consistency, and uncomplicated solutions at little cost or risk. It wins when we produce policies with irreconcilable mandates both to protect principal and to buy securities that do not protect principal. We want it both ways, but we can't have it.

The army of wishful thinking wields a subtle weapon: American competitiveness. From little league to college business class, Americans are taught either to compete themselves or to support a team. We love the home team, the products of our company, our fraternity/sorority, or a host of other familiar groups. We do not spend time deciding which team to support. We do not study data, evaluate and embrace a hypothesis, and establish selection criteria. Instead, we support a comfortable choice, the one we know best from our family, neighborhood, political, or business experiences, and we want our team to beat others even if victory produces few benefits.

In carrying out their obligation to select money managers, trustees participate in investment competition. They are judges; they determine who wins! Ideally, choices are not based on one-time "beauty contests," but on philosophy and precedent, risk and reward, vision and policy, and the self-evident truths—all supported by portfolio theory. These are weapons of the small platoon of ideas that wins when trustees write effective policies and hire money managers according to the needs of their organization.

Yet competition is useful. Recognizing that boards of trustees and their committees are parts of a competitive fabric, the investment community has produced dozens of different methods to define investment strategies and to measure results. The language of modern investing developed from these efforts. For example, one equity strategy, called *growth,* has teams grouped according to "styles" such as asset allocation, market timing, and fundamental analysis. The *fixed income* strategy is played in leagues called credit quality, duration, average life, and active or passive management. Other strategies are *venture capital, managed futures, real estate, international, structured investments, hedge funds,* and *portfolio immunization.* Trustees must be aware of these and other techniques that have improved understanding of investment phenomena—and helped investors to make money.

Regulators, professional associations, periodicals, and consulting firms observe the competition and collect results. They define the rules, help establish categories, place investment firms in a category, and determine who has done best. Unfortunately, there is nothing simple about these calculations, for results can be presented in different ways. First, there are infinite intervals to compare and wide disagreement about which is best. Some say it is best to compare managers over a market cycle, but both popular and professional periodicals usually report results over more widely understood periods such as quarters, years, five-year periods, and decades. Also, competitors can be compared either directly or within plan sponsor categories. In the first method, data services compare all growth managers; in the second, growth managers serving endowments are compared to other growth managers serving endowments, pension managers to pension managers, museum endowment managers to other museum endowment managers, and so forth. If the World Series were this complicated, no one would watch, but trustees need to watch. They articulate a vision, choose the game, select teams to support, make changes if necessary, and live with results. This is implementation. This is what trustees do.

Policy implementation is manager selection. To select managers, trustees build perspective about hundreds of different ideas employed by professional investors. Trustees learn the theories and jargon before meeting investment managers during interviews. It is like searching for a new automobile. One person starts in the showroom where an effective salesperson points out "the car of your dreams" that must be purchased right now before someone else gets it. Another person, however, uses a different approach, analyzing family needs and requirements for efficiency and luxury. By reading consumer magazines and newspaper advertisements, this person gains perspective on price and then decides how much to spend. This person knows what to buy, and will find the appropriate auto at a fair price. He is a *trustee* of his affairs and would be a good trustee of other people's money—because he prepares.

Trustees are prepared when they not only *think* that risk and reward are related but really *believe* it. They have resolved that the platoon of ideas is more useful than the army of aspirations and wishful thinking, and they have subordinated competitive energy to comprehensive understanding of their organization's vision.

Given time and effort, anyone can appreciate investment theory and acquire perspective on risk and value. We seek a general awareness of investments similar to the awareness of a golfer who properly evaluates distance, elevation, wind, and personal skills to reach the cup. In investing, the important elements are price, diversification, direction, and time. We become aware by observing debates between professional investors. Let's assume there are two debate teams, one from Common Sense University, the other from the College of Mathematical Models. The following is the opening statement from Common Sense, whose captain is the legendary Peter Lynch, former manager of the Fidelity Magellan Fund:

> Twenty years in this business convinces me that any normal person using the customary three percent of the brain can pick stocks just as well, if not better, than the average Wall Street expert. . . . There's a famous story about a fireman from New England. Apparently back in the 1950s he couldn't help noticing that [a local factory] was expanding at a furious pace. It occurred to him that they wouldn't be expanding so fast unless they were prospering, and on that assumption he and his family invested $2,000. Not only that, they put in another $2,000 each year for the next five years. By 1972 the fireman was a millionaire. . . . I get many of [my investment ideas] the way the fireman got his. I talk to hundreds of companies a year and spend hour after hour in heady powwows with CEOs, financial

analysts, and my colleagues in the mutual-fund business, but I stumble onto the big winners in extracurricular situations, the same way [anyone] could.[1]

Peter Lynch is a "fundamentalist," an investor who looks directly at the circumstances and prospects of a business. Simplistically, a fundamentalist invests in companies with customers lined up around the block and executives who realistically manage growth. Mr. Lynch demonstrated a superior ability to find profitable companies by looking at fundamentals. Therefore, his words communicate both slight disdain for "technicians," who spend hours studying the economy or charts of price movements, and conviction that anyone can find value using "three percent of the brain."

Another famous proponent of common sense is Sir John Templeton, who has served public investors since 1940 through the Templeton Family of mutual funds. Here is what he says:

> After 49 years of professional investment counseling worldwide, I believe that successful investing is mainly common sense. It is common sense to search for an asset where you can buy the *greatest value for each dollar you pay*. This means bargain hunting. . . . *To diversify your investments* is clearly common sense so that those which produce more profits than expected will offset those which produce less. Even the best investment professional must expect that no more than two thirds of his decisions will prove to be above average in profits. . . . It is only common sense *to prepare for a bear market*. Experts do not know when each bear market will begin, but you can be certain that there will be many bear markets during your lifetime. Common sense investing means that you should prepare yourself [for declining markets] both financially and *psychologically*.[2] (All emphasis added.)

Of course, professionals in any field have a comprehensive common sense that is difficult for others to acquire. A professional athlete working eight hours a day naturally gains greater appreciation for the techniques and requirements of his sport than does the amateur. In fact, the knowledge and experience of professionals is so comprehensive that often their greatest personal challenge is to tolerate lesser capabilities in others. This is self-confidence that sometimes offends. Though never publicly stated, the greatest investors, sincerely believing their work is comprehensible, often think to themselves, This is easy, and you ought to be able to do it, too, or at least to understand what I do.[3] In reality, trustees rarely acquire a broad perspective on investment value because they work in other fields. Hence, they hire money managers.

The College of Mathematical Models presents a different view. Its team captain, a "technician,"[4] opens debate this way:

> We believe every phenomenon is effectively understood by translating its characteristics into numbers, then analyzing those numbers. Furthermore, we hypothecate that rapid screening of numbers by computer is most likely to reveal important trends and unusual opportunities.
>
> Although our thesis defends thousands of models created by different individuals with different criteria and temperaments, our approach in general will produce superior returns because it is continuous and consistent. Mechanical analysis of statistics is reliable; it is not subject to vacations, daily variations in personal energy, or even changes in criteria or attitude caused by emotion, aging, illness and the like. We also believe that mathematical modeling is not a luxury. It is a necessity because individuals cannot assimilate all information presented by modern life. Finally, our techniques will faithfully and consistently carry out written investment policies.

Fundamental and technical analysis (Common Sense University and the University of Mathematical Models, respectively) include subcategories, which are listed in Table 11–1. Consultants and financial periodicals define the categories. However, the definitions are so imprecise that it is difficult for most money managers to explain what they do and how they do it. For example, John Templeton states that he searches for bargains worldwide, but he neither provides a definition of *bargain* nor describes his method of searching. Such imprecision and uncertainty frustrate trustees and lead to inconsistent investment programs. This is why trustees must both *believe* that growth occurs naturally in an expanding economy and embrace general principles of investing. It is like commissioning an artist. Those who finance the creation of art *believe* it is feasible to produce something beautiful, but they do not know *for sure!* They proceed on faith, knowing only the artist's style and reputation.

MODERN PORTFOLIO THEORY

In addition to having faith, intuitive understanding of risk and reward, and knowledge of investment strategy categories created by those who measure results, trustees also should know *modern portfolio theory (MPT),*[5] the most important intellectual tool for contemporary investors.

TABLE 11–1
Alternative Styles

A. Equity Styles

Fundamental *(Common Sense;* *Analysis of Accounting* *Statements)*	*Technical* *(Mathematical Models;* *Analysis of Price* *and Volume)*

I. **Value***
II. **Growth***
III. Yield
IV. **Top-down**
V. **Bottom-up**
VI. Equity/cash allocators
VII. **Market-oriented**
VIII. **Price-driven**
IX. **Rotators***
	I. **Timers**
	  1. Predict market trend by observing and defining recent market trends.
	  2. Predict industry or specific stock trends by observing actual recent price changes.
	  3. Predict market, industry, or stock trends using modified data such as **moving averages** or **relative strength.**
	II. Computer **screeners**
	  1. Earnings quality
	  2. Earnings momentum
	  3. Minimums such as book value, PE, or proprietary criteria.

B. Debt[†] Styles

Fundamental	*Technical*
I. **Cash:** short maturities, usually less than one year. II. Intermediate: 2- to 15-year maturities. III. Long term: 10- to 40-year bonds. IV. **Core:** well-known bonds usually laddered.	I. Anticipators (of changes in interest rates) predict bond prices analyzing interest rate trends and economic models. II. Stated **duration** managers meet duration criteria set by sponsor. III. **Index** managers try to match results of an index.

C. Types of Managers

Hedge Fund Managers

Hedge fund managers seek to reduce risk by utilizing options and financial futures contracts and by buying **long** and selling **short** to reduce risk of loss. Generally, gains also are limited when hedging techniques are applied.

Arbitrage Managers

Arbitrage managers seek to exploit values that arise between similar securities listed on different exchanges, securities of companies being acquired by other companies, and specific stocks or *indexes* and their related *warrants,* options or futures contracts.

TABLE 11–1 (*continued*)

Index Managers

Utilizing computers, **index** *managers* attempt to duplicate the exact performance of an index by actually purchasing securities used to calculate the index. (Some managers attempt to duplicate indexes by using only a sample of stocks in the index or by purchasing option or futures contracts.)

Contrarian Managers

"The best time to buy a straw hat is in winter," an old market saying, is the credo of the contrarian. **Contrarian** *managers* (equity and debt) purchase out-of-favor securities, such as savings and loan stocks during their financial crisis, bonds and preferred stocks behind on payments, or securities issued in Chile during political turmoil. They assume that bargains appear during crises.

---

*Rotators are found in both value and growth styles
†Often called *fixed income* because payments on most debt instruments are fixed.

Definitions of boldfaced words appear in the glossary either independently or under *styles*.

An investment committee's most important job is to choose money managers. Choice requires categorization. (It is impossible to acquire anything without first selecting a category, as in, "I want a small, two-door automobile with automatic transmission.") Categories of private investment managers are known as styles. Styles began as self-described marketing labels to distinguish one manager from another. Now, independent consultants both define styles and assign managers to style categories.

This table catalogs styles. The definitions are mine. Different consultants use different definitions. Therefore, trustees should avoid confusion by utilizing information from one consultant only.

Any domestic or international manager, whether fundamental or technical, may concentrate on companies that have (1) *large cap* (large capitalization; usually older companies that have grown large with time) or (2) *small cap* (small capitalization; usually younger firms in new industries, sometimes called emerging growth).

Any of the above styles can be applied globally (purchasing securities from both the United States and other nations) or internationally (only other nations or geographic regions).

(concluded)

MPT is neither a theory nor is it modern, but it does formally recognize the trade-off between risk and return. Its focus is portfolios, not individual securities. It is a body of thought and principles that serves as a practical point of departure for creating policy and designing a total investment program. This is asset allocation. Although based in descriptive mathematical models that began to appear in the 1950s, its general principles are both compelling and easy to understand. Every trustee should be familiar with them.

MPT assumes that investors create portfolios instead of purchasing individual securities. It also proposes that individuals are risk averse and that they therefore diversify instinctively. To explain this tendency to diversify, MPT provides tools to measure both risk and reward. It then further suggests that the risk of an entire portfolio depends on the interaction among its constituent securities. If one security rises at the same rate another falls, the net is no change at all, assuming both are equally weighted. If one category of securities such as oil stocks appreciates while another such as utilities declines, the total change in portfolio value is small. In other words, if two different risk assets tend to change in price counter to one another, the total risk of a portfolio containing both is less than each asset standing alone. Of course, this supports our intuitive belief that diversification reduces risk, but it also reveals new perspectives. One is that it is possible to reduce the risk of an entire portfolio by introducing an asset that itself has high risk, provided that the new asset tends to move counter to other assets in the portfolio. Another new perspective is that trustees can create a portfolio with measurable risk.

To achieve understanding of risk and reward, MPT applied statistical tools. These include beta and standard deviation (measuring risk), total return (reward), and covariance (the statistical correlation revealing how one group of securities has moved relative to another). For trustees, covariance is the most important tool because it describes *relative* historic changes in prices of marketable securities. Investment committees can use covariance to allocate assets because it demonstrates how one asset class has interacted with another.

An important function of investment policy is to allocate assets. *Asset allocation* is another term whose meaning varies with usage. We use it to describe how trustees divide funds between debt and equity securities, and between subcategories such as international, venture capital, real estate, and so forth.[6] Unfortunately, the term also has been adopted by money management firms to imply a distinctive investment style. The distinction is blurry, however, because firms allocate in different universes. If the universe is stocks, managers allocate among industries or among segments such as early-cycle and late-cycle stocks. If the universe is bonds, allocation occurs by maturity or duration, or even between government bonds and corporate bonds. In other words, the term *asset al-*

location is inadequate to describe an investment management style. On the other hand, asset allocation is a significant investment committee function. It is the search for the ideal investment program.

Modern portfolio theory describes an "efficient" portfolio as a mixture of stocks, bonds, and cash with the greatest potential reward for a given theoretical risk. (MPT does not suggest that an efficient portfolio will give the greatest total return. Great results always have been achieved by concentrating capital in "inefficient," speculative categories or in strategies that have an unusually high possibility of loss. Instead, MPT suggests that there is a measurable level of risk for each level of expected return.) A popular allocation among income-oriented endowment funds is 60 percent debt securities and 40 percent equities. Pension funds have tended toward a 50/50 mix. In each case, committees believe they have designed a theoretically efficient portfolio, the ideal split between debt and equity. Although it is useful to use modern portfolio theory in this way, there are two unfortunate consequences. The first is that committees try to design ideal portfolios instead of investment plans appropriate to their organizations. Instead of discussing vision and goals, trustees debate the 60/40 split.

You can hear the debate: "I move that we allocate 60 percent to bonds and 40 percent to stocks," says trustee number one. Number two then says, "But I think we can afford more risk. How about 50 percent stocks, 50 percent bonds?" This continues until compromise is reached.

A second consequence is that MPT limits meeting agendas. It creates the premise, and committees do not debate other possibilities. In the perfect system of governance, committees would consider *all* possibilities, including unusual proposals such as allocating 100 percent to small cap stocks worldwide, but committees seldom hear aggressive proposals because they *assume* the task is to allocate among different asset classes. Committees fear creating inefficient investment programs as defined by modern portfolio theory. The 60/40, or 50/50, or 70/30 idea has become so powerful that it inhibits creative thought in committees trying to achieve compromise. A frequent result is dull policy.[7]

THE POWER OF POLICY

Whether stimulating or dull, policy determines portfolio performance. In two widely quoted studies, authors Gary Brinson, Brian Singer, and

Gilbert Beebower conclude that investment policy has a greater impact on portfolio performance than active asset allocation or security selection. In other words, the basic policy structure imposed by trustees is the most important determinant of portfolio performance. Here is what they say:

> Specifically, data from 82 large pension plans over the 1977–87 period indicate that *investment policy* explained, on average, 91.5 per cent of the variation in quarterly total plan returns.[8]

This study assumed that there are three elements in the portfolio process:

1. Investment policy: "specification of the plan sponsor's objectives, constraints and requirements, including identification of the normal asset allocation mix."[9]
2. Active asset allocation: "temporarily deviating from the policy asset mix in order to benefit from a state of capital market disequilibrium with respect to the investment fundamentals underlying the policy mix."[10]
3. Security selection: investment decisions to purchase or sell specific stocks and bonds.

After mathematically analyzing data supplied by consultant SEI Corporation, the authors were convinced that "the overwhelming factor in determining the basic, long-term return achieved per unit of risk was investment policy."[11]

In the context of organizational governance, it probably makes little difference whether policy affects 91.5 percent, 65 percent, or only 30 percent of quarterly variations. No matter how it is viewed or what magnitude of influence it is believed to have, policy powerfully impacts results. Policy is made by trustees. It is the efficiency and effectiveness of investment committees—their capacity to create and clearly state investment policy—that has the greatest single impact on an organization's future financial health. Therefore, committees should give more time to policy creation than to any other investment function, more than they give to hiring managers and consultants, reviewing results, or evaluating the economy.

APPLYING THEORY

How do committees apply theory? The following is a practical path to successful implementation.

**Long-Term Returns
(25 Years Ending 1991)**

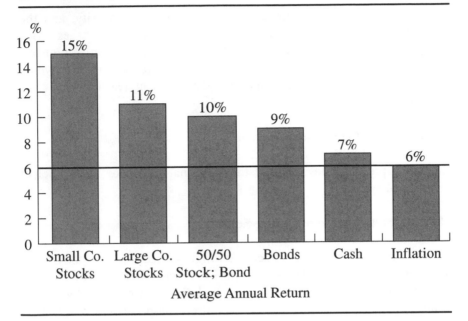

Long-term returns show the power of policy. Over this 25-year period, trustees who placed 100 percent in small-company stocks would have earned 50 percent more per year than the more common 50/50 stock/bond split.

Meeting One (Getting To Know You)

Trustees build rapport with one another by self-introductions and sharing personal experiences. (In some cultures, relationships are more important than tasks. In ours, tasks are most important, but people who know and like each other do best.)

Meeting Two (Down to Business)

Review goals and vision of the organization. Keep them in view at all times. Designate a consultant. (Every committee has a consultant, the person who makes things happen. The investment committee's consultant may be a committee member, a staff officer, or a professional.) Create a vision for the investment committee, and prepare specific and measurable investment goals—in writing.

Meeting Three (Theory)

Review modern portfolio theory, Common Sense University, and the University of Mathematical Models. Be sure the policy expresses a risk assumption. Select strategies from Table 11–1. Establish an administrative procedure for hiring money managers and for determining which managers the committee will interview. Consider the feasibility of visiting offices of managers.

Meeting Four (The Beauty Pageant)

Listen to presentations by investment managers. Take notes. Select money managers.

Meeting Five (Now It's Getting Serious)

Sign money management contracts. Arrange for securities custody, trading, performance evaluations, and proxy voting. Talk informally with new managers. Try rapport building techniques. Conclude by telling managers about the vision and goals of both the committee and the entire organization.

* * * * *

There is one other method to carry out policy: Find people instead of strategies. Superlative investment portfolios are more the products of great investors than of great ideas. We know great investors retrospec-tively—Keynes, Baruch, Rowe Price, Graham, Templeton, Buffett, Lynch, and many others—but how do we find them prospectively? How can a plan sponsor retain an investor who is not yet great?

In two books of interviews with more than 17 great investors, John Train found that they have the following common personal characteristics:

1. They are realistic. "The mind is balanced; it works well, like a watch."[12]
2. They are "intelligent to the point of genius."[13]
3. If not geniuses, they are utterly dedicated to their craft. Often they have an "overwhelming competitive instinct." Many started life poor and thereby developed an intense personal desire for financial security. They are "prodigiously well in

THE MANAGER PARADE: HOW TO MINIMIZE TIME SPENT ON MANAGER SEARCHES

Ward Cammack, managing director of Investment Management Evaluation Service (IMES), synthesized the following ideas at a national conference of endowment and foundation trustees and executives. They appear here with his permission.*

Committees Retain Managers for the Wrong Reasons. What Are Those Reasons?

1. Manager has an in-law on the board.
2. Backstudy shows that a manager has beaten a benchmark, such as an index, by a wide margin, and trustees believe the manager can sustain that record.
3. Board equates average performance with conservatism.
4. "Goliath Asset Management" is hired because board believes its size is a sign of conservatism.
5. Groupthink. Everyone hires everyone else's manager.
6. The board is attracted to the "product du jour," a recently successful style, such as small cap (1983), real estate (1985), international (1987), short funds (1990), bio tech (1992).

Time Wasters

1. Evaluating managers that don't fit the fund's strategy.
2. "Excruciating" examination of short-term performance; a long, detailed review of performance statistics.
3. Hours spent listening to managers discuss economic outlook, current investment tactics, and reasons for purchasing a specific security.
4. Interviewing last year's winners, the owners of the product du jour.

Protect the Fund

1. Set specific criteria and stick to them.
2. Keep one eye on the vision and the investment policy.
3. Focus on people, philosophy, process, product.
4. Put your mind at ease.
   a. No one consistently predicts the economy or the markets correctly.
   b. No single philosophy prevails in all markets. (Diversify!)
   c. You invest in an unknown future, not the present or the past. The future is a mystery, and the road to it has chuckholes. If you hit one, just fix the tire.

THE MANAGER PARADE: (*continued*)

3. For superior performance, do not hire managers frequently retained by sister institutions.

4. Work from the bottom up. Establish your criteria, and find managers that fit. Do not allow either a manager's style or charisma to define your policies.
   a. Establish the structure or framework to invest.
   b. Hire a manager for a specific task within the structure.
   c. Remember that there is no manager for all seasons.

Important Questions to Ask Managers

1. What makes a security attractive to you?
2. What causes you to buy a security? What causes you to sell?
3. How many securities do you own at any one time?
4. Do you maintain cash? Is the level of cash a function of timing?
5. Who in your organization makes decisions?
6. Have you ever changed your style or process?
7. Tell us about your staff. Who was hired when and why? Has anyone left your firm in the last five years?
8. How do you motivate your staff?
9. Who owns the firm?
10. After each presentation, trustees should ask:
    a. Does it make sense?
    b. Does it fit our structure?
    c. Can I/we explain the manager's process in five minutes or less?

Managing the Manager Parade†

1. Allow 15 minutes between presentations to discuss and review notes.

2. Schedule a 15-minute relaxation break every 90 minutes. Avoid fatigue.

3. Plan two hours to make the final choice. Make the decision right after the presentations. Do not wait!

---

*IMES is a division of Equitable Securities Corporation. It is located at 800 Nashville City Center, P.O. Box 2727, Nashville, TN 37219

†The manager parade is a series of scheduled interviews to select an investment manager.

(*concluded*)

formed" and work hard; their "eyes glitter" when they talk about their work.[14]

4. They are "disciplined and patient." They abandon unattainable objectives while sticking to their ideas and procedures. "If you don't know and aren't disciplined, you risk getting shaken out just at the wrong time, like the bird that bursts from cover at the approach of the hunter."[15]

5. They are loners. "The loner's truth is within himself, while his opposite, the externalizer, is constantly testing the reaction of others and positioning himself in relation to them—usually to enjoy their esteem, but sometimes to express hostility. All great leaders, artists, and thinkers have to be loners; it's often very hard to keep them on the team."[16]

Investment committees could search for individuals with these and other important personal characteristics. In place of receiving proposals and watching the "parade of managers" (a series of interviews over one or two days), committees could actively search and recruit. This is a different way of looking at the hiring process. It proposes that trustees create lines of communication or networks through which they identify outstanding individuals who might become outstanding professional investors because they have skills and aptitudes similar to those of great investors of the past. This active search for money management talent would require both a new attitude and new commitment from trustees more accustomed to listening than to recruiting. The effort would be time-consuming, but financial rewards would be great for any institution that finds the next great investor.

NOTES

1. Peter Lynch, *One Up on Wall Street,* (New York: Simon & Schuster, 1989), pp. 13, 18.
2. Quoted in Roger C. Gibson, *Asset Allocation* (Homewood, Ill.: Dow Jones-Irwin, 1990), pp. xi–xiv.
3. Perhaps arrogance is a plus in hiring money managers.
4. Nobel laureates Harry M. Markowitz, William F. Sharpe, and Merton H. Miller are "technicians" because they work with mathematical tools. The word *technician* also is applied to strategists who anticipate market moves by studying either charts and graphs or current prices compared to long-term average prices.

5. I use the term *modern portfolio theory* in the broadest possible sense to include related concepts such as the capital asset pricing model.
6. Some plan sponsors hire professionals to allocate assets, but I believe most investment committees do it themselves by directly hiring managers who have different styles.
7. Investment concepts seem to have a self-destruct mechanism—popularity. When many investors use the same concept, its results become average. MPT will survive, but its applications will change. Probably, smart investors already are testing new applications and making money, but we will not hear about them until success is proved. Then we will try their methods. Everyone will try them, and results again will gravitate to average.
8. Gary P. Brinson, Brian D. Singer, and Gilbert L. Beebower, "Determinants of Portfolio Performance II: An Update," *The Financial Analysts Journal*, May–June 1991, p. 40ff.
9. Ibid.
10. Ibid.
11. Ibid.
12. John Train, *The Money Masters*, (New York: Harper & Row, 1980), pp. 213–15.
13. Ibid.
14. Ibid.
15. Ibid.
16. Ibid.

CHAPTER 12

COMMUNICATIONS ON BOARDS AND INVESTMENT COMMITTEES

This is a story about four people named Everybody, Somebody, Anybody, and Nobody. There was an important job to be done, and Everybody was sure Somebody would do it. Anybody could have done it, but Nobody did it. Somebody got angry, because it was Everybody's job. Everybody thought Anybody could to it, but Nobody realized Everybody wouldn't do it. So Everybody blamed Somebody when Nobody did what Anybody could have done!

Anonymous

Imagine a fund for which no one is responsible. The board of directors is legally accountable for the $10 million Ancestry Foundation of Grapefruit County. It has appointed an investment committee composed of the county's leading professional investors and investment bankers, but none concurrently serve on the board of directors. Furthermore, no board member is a member of the investment committee, although the board chairperson sits ex officio.

The investment committee meets four times a year, usually late in the afternoon. No one has elected or appointed a committee chairperson, but a consensus exists that Bill Brokerhaven, the oldest among them, is spokesperson. Committee meetings are informal, and most commence with conversations about local politics, companies, and personnel changes, as well as recent corporate and municipal financings and national legislation or regulations affecting their businesses. During the last 30 minutes, the committee does make an asset allocation recommendation to the board's professional investment advisor, George Trustworthy, who records his interpretation of the instructions and returns to his office to carry them out. The investment committee adjourns.

Meanwhile, the advisor meets twice a year with the board of directors, giving a detailed report on rates of return. Usually, quoted returns are in line with recent averages, which is never good enough for one board member, who himself is a professional investor but not a member of the investment committee. He interrogates George Trustworthy, often challenging the wisdom of individual security choices. The questioning is particularly harsh in years when common stocks have not generated a positive return. Often, George leaves the room believing that no one supports his actions.

In this hypothetical circumstance, the investment committee has no legal connection to the board and makes no written recommendations to the board, but only makes suggestions to the advisor, who records, interprets, and carries out those suggestions without formal direction from the board. The board never records its own points of view, policies, goals, and investment results, and it leaves specific decisions to the investment advisor, George Trustworthy, who feels no personal satisfaction from this work and does not have the slightest idea who his boss is. He is frustrated by the interrogations and the criticism he receives for carrying out asset allocation decisions that were made by the invisible investment committee. He prefers to work on other accounts that respect his decisions, which in fact is what he does. The results: mediocre returns for the Ancestry Foundation and less financial support for Grapefruit County projects.

Inefficient organization, poor communications, and normal human deficiencies directly contribute to below-average investment returns for thousands of plan sponsors every year. The Ancestry Foundation, for example, has given no attention to its hierarchy; no one knows who should report to whom. The following is a list of similarly self-destructive circumstances.

1. Administration of a company retirement plan is delegated to the controller, whose primary job is to keep the company's accounts. Therefore, the new assignment is a personal burden. It will require extra hours without extra compensation or personal recognition. The controller is not enthusiastic.

2. A charitable organization believes its investment program is inefficient. The board asks certain officers to resolve the problem, and it seems important that all are involved. Unfortunately, it is difficult to schedule meetings everyone can attend; only two occur the first year. The treasurer agrees to draft an investment policy. He develops his draft by referring to policies in textbooks. The draft is approved, but investment advisors later state that it is impossible to fulfill all of the requirements of the policy, especially the social responsibility criterion, forcing reconsideration at the next board meeting two months later. The policy is finally approved two years after the need was felt, and it takes three additional months to carry it out. The organization does not realize even average returns for more than two years.

3. From proposal to closing, it takes over nine months for Company A to acquire Company B. The individual responsible for Company B's employee benefit plan resigns immediately, knowing that his job will be eliminated. The president of company B says that he will handle the plan, but in fact he ignores it in favor of more pressing administrative issues. Company A presumes that Company B's plan will be merged with its own, but the merger of the two plans is a low-priority, time-consuming bureaucratic process. Therefore, no one supervises the plan and a treasurer places new contributions in short-term, low-yield money market instruments. This continues more than a year after the acquisition is closed because everyone says, "Let's not do anything until regulators approve merger of the retirement plans." The result: poor investment returns. (Qualified retirement plan assets should be managed at all times; until a merger is complete, the assets in each should be managed separately.)

4. A new college president wants to spend more endowment funds on plant and equipment. In his view, the college will not attract good students without these improvements. He also feels that physical facilities such as dormitories and classrooms are investments like stocks and bonds because they potentially reduce costs through efficiency and might grow in value. He wants the investment committee to agree to this new spending policy. However, the committee's policy is to build future income by spending less today. Trustees on the committee are volunteers from all over the United States who meet infrequently. Feeling urgency, the president cancels a contract with the investment consultant hired by the committee and assigns a new staff person to supervise. The investment committee chairperson resists these changes and asks for a special meeting, but conflicting schedules make it impossible to meet for three months. Although existing money managers continue to manage the endowment, new funds received from the president's capital improvement campaign are not permanently invested. In all, it takes more than 18 months to resolve the dispute, partly because documents and minutes do not clearly specify who can make final decisions for the endowment.

Another useful perspective has been provided by Arthur Williams III in his book *Managing Your Investment Manager.* Williams develops a concept called "The Utility of the People Responsible for the Fund."

This concept reveals those elements of personal perspective that retard progress. Mr. Williams's narrative presents the reflections of five individuals involved with a company retirement plan:

Member of Board of Directors: Since I'm nearing retirement age, any benefit to the company achieved from having an aggressive policy will be achieved long after I am gone. Therefore, I will tend toward a conservative policy to eliminate any problems that might disrupt my last years with the company.

Pension Director: In terms of progressing within this company, the chances of helping my career by taking big risks in the fund seem to be much less than the chances of hurting my career by being unsuccessful in a high-risk policy. This leads me to be conservative. However, if I do an especially good job here, other, larger companies might hire me to oversee their funds. Perhaps I should be more aggressive.

Investment Manager: If I am not at all imaginative in running this fund, the chances are I will keep the business and manage more each year due to growth while possibly picking up occasional new contributions, which means the assets under my management will grow. However, if I take more risks and show better returns, I may be able to build a name for myself and my organization, and attract more new clients.

Actuary: If I am conservative in my assumptions, the company probably will not have to increase its contributions over and above my estimates, and plan participants will be highly likely to receive their benefits. On the other hand, the company may wish to reduce its current contributions in order to increase its net income, which can be done if I choose less conservative assumptions. Perhaps my firm will be replaced if I am not aggressive enough.

Company Shareholder: I don't want the company to run awry of ERISA or have to make excessive contributions due to poor investment results. However, the greater the return we can get on fund assets, the lower the contributions will be and hence the higher my stock price and dividends.[1]

The "utility" of individuals on boards of foundations and endowments is more complex, for these persons must consider their roles and status in the community at large. Many believe that appointment to a board and its committees is a seal of approval for the local or national status they wish to maintain. They also know that other board members with equal status will evaluate the personal skills they demonstrate during meetings. The chief executive officer (CEO) of one company will evaluate the CEO of another, and important business relationships occasionally start from board-generated friendships. Clearly, these individuals are unlikely to launch a creative boat, to change existing business relationships, to dismiss old friends, or to advocate aggressive policy. Instead, they prefer to wait for consensus.

Trustees also give little attention to *effective governance,* a phrase synonymous with good communications. In their book, *Fortune & Folly: The Wealth & Power of Institutional Investing,* authors William M. O'Barr and John M. Conley affirm this proposition. They say:

> Our larger point relates to the concept of *discipline,* a word currently in vogue in the investment world. Pension fund executives talk constantly about the discipline that results from having committees reassess asset allocation decisions, or from evaluating outside managers against relevant benchmarks. Yet there seems to be little discipline imposed on the most basic undertaking of all: shaping the entity that will be responsible for the money. It seems not to have occurred to the people who run pension funds that they lack discipline in this area, or that it could benefit them as much as they believe it does in other, less consequential areas. Reasonable minds might differ on what form this discipline should take, but it seems beyond dispute that some form of conscious, disciplined analysis is in order.[2]

This is to say that trustees and staff should exert as much effort evaluating themselves as they do evaluating money managers. They should create discipline, good communication, and strong governance.

(Of the tens of thousands of individuals who have served voluntarily on investment committees, it is curious that none has written comprehensively about the experience. Instead, books are written by observers, including money managers and consultants, staff officers such as treasurers and controllers, and academics. This gap in the literature could reflect lack of interest, issue avoidance, fear of offending, feelings of helplessness, or unwillingness to express strong points of view.)

*   *   *   *   *

Clogged communications arteries of governing bodies cause governance attacks. Symptoms are lack of enthusiasm and delay. The result is poor investment performance—fewer financial resources for future good work. Just as cholesterol forms arteriosclerotic plaques, personal competition, vague job descriptions, blurred lines of authority, and ambiguous hierarchical arrangements impede both understanding and progress. Arthur Williams III concurs by saying, "Although the consideration of these utility factors is potentially embarrassing . . . , failure to consider them can be disastrous for the fund."[3]

Williams's reference to *disaster* is itself intriguing. The word could refer to a calamitous event, such as the stock market decline of October 1987, or to specific investments that default, enter bankruptcy, or lose market value. These occurrences stimulate action in any investment committee. They give rise to an immediate need. Unfortunately, the most important investment disaster does not produce immediate action because it is not felt in the present. This is loss of a future opportunity.

While individuals act quickly and decisively on current personal and business needs such as housing, transportation, health and entertainment, manufacturing inefficiencies or declining earnings, they do not act promptly to manage future needs like retirement, children's education, estate planning, or continuity of business management. This is why investment committees move slowly. Members do not *feel* urgency because both potential benefits and disasters occur in the distant future. Nevertheless, the costs of delay and poor management are staggering. Table 12–1 reveals some potential costs of delay. Costs of poor management are revealed by computing the 1992 value of $1 invested at year-end 1925 in different asset classes. The values are:

1. Treasury bills: $11.40.
2. Long-term government bonds: $23.71.
3. Common stocks: $727.38.
4. Small stocks: $2,279.04.[4]

These differences are huge, and it may be only a minor exaggeration to state that trustees who did not earn the greater returns did cause disaster.

Subtle, invisible, insidious governance attacks that cause consequential loss of future opportunities are avoided by (1) good communications; (2) a clear vision and clear goals; (3) an established, written line of authority; and (4) a prearranged method to make quick decisions or to deal with crises. Having these elements of governance in place leads to enthusiasm, confidence, accomplishment, and a personal sense of reward. These four factors are defined below.

TABLE 12–1
The Cost of Delay (Earnings on $100,000)

Opportunity Cost		Future Value* of $ Lost		
Rate	$ Lost In 1 Year	10 years	20 years	30 years
3%	$ 3,000	$ 4,031.75	$ 5,418.33	$ 7,281.79
5	5,000	8,144.47	13,266.49	21,609.71
10	10,000	25,937.42	67,275.00	174,494.02

*Assumes compounding once each year at the same rate lost the first year.

The cost of delay is opportunity lost. It is the difference between a rate earned and a rate that could have been earned through a different investment decision. For example, if a treasurer places funds in short-term deposits or money funds yielding 3 percent, but could have earned 6 percent in a bond fund, the opportunity cost is 3 percent. (But note that opportunity cost varies dramatically from year to year, and from asset class to asset class.)

   In other words, if an investment committee could have earned an *additional* 5 percent by investing $100,000 at the beginning of a year instead of the end of a year, it would have provided $21,609.71 more resources for beneficiaries 30 years hence. (This is the future value of $5,000 compounded at 5 percent.) If the amount under management is $10 million instead of $100,000, the additional value in 30 years is $4,321,942.37. If the delay in obtaining a higher rate of return is more than one year, the opportunity cost increases rapidly.

Good Communications

An easy rapport exists between committee members. During meetings, every idea is expressed. There are no bad ideas. Consultants and advisors are treated equally with members; they have no fear that presenting a new idea might result in termination of their contracts. No one dominates or intimidates. Although roles are defined (chairperson, secretary, heads of specific projects), everyone feels equal to everyone else. Paid staff members are consulted, and their views respected.

Vision and Goals

Four documents are visible to all committee members: the vision and goals of the organization, and the vision and goals of the investment committee. They appear either on the wall of the committee meeting room or as the first inserts of the committee's agenda book.

Established Lines of Authority

The board of directors has specifically delegated and described the goals, responsibilities, and powers of the investment committee. This data appears in the minutes. The investment committee chairperson knows to whom he or she must report. The committee vice chairperson may act in the chairperson's absence. Any member of the committee or the board may propose action on short notice, and decisions may be reached by telephone conference call. A quorum is defined. The authority of important third parties who are not members of the investment committee (such as university presidents, foundation executive directors, company presidents, and chief financial officers) is specified in writing, and they are permitted to make certain decisions (probably relating to staff and consultants). Consultants have received letters outlining their responsibilities and explaining to whom they must report. Money managers have received similar information, including how the committee views the role of the consultants.

Expedited Decisions

Committee documents contain a decision-making procedure to be utilized when delay would cost money. Circumstances include receipt of a large unexpected donation, dramatic changes in the market or national economy, the incapacity of an important consultant or money manager, or a request for clarification of policy by a money manager or a professional proposal to invest in a unique security such as a private placement. The printed procedure describes which committee officers should initiate discussions, how fax machines and conference calls should be used, and what to do if an important committee member or professional is not available. (If the committee is dealing in an atmosphere of crisis, such as the stock market decline of 1987, the procedure should require committee members to gain perspective before making a final decision. This is achieved by mandating a careful review of similar past crises over a 24-hour cooling off period between initial discussion of a proposal and the final decision.)

No investment committee operates with all these benefits, and some operate with none. Nevertheless, all investment committees should attempt to clear their communications arteries so that information flows quickly and comfortably. Occasionally, committees must retain outside consultants to both demonstrate need for change and to prescribe how to do it.

NOTES

1. Arthur Williams III, *Managing Your Investment Manager*, (Homewood Ill.: Business One Irwin, 1986), pp. 38–40.
2. William M. O'Barr and John M. Conley, *Fortune & Folly: The Wealth & Power of Institutional Investing*, (Homewood, Ill.: Business One Irwin, 1992), p. 71.
3. Williams, *Managing Your Investment Manager*, p. 40.
4. Ibbotson Associates, Inc., *Stocks, Bonds, Bills, and Inflation 1993 Yearbook*, p. 28.

CHAPTER 13

CRISES

Great occasions do not make heroes or cowards; they simply unveil them to the eyes of men. Silently and imperceptibly, as we wake or sleep, we grow strong or we grow weak, and at last some crisis shows us what we have become.

Bishop Westcott

As individuals and as trustees, investors face crises that are either obvious or subtle. Obvious crises include unanticipated events such as market crashes, deaths of leaders, terrorism, and war. Even expected events, such as the inauguration of leaders or promulgation of laws, give rise to both emotions and decisions. Trustees must respond promptly to these obvious changes, as well as to changes in their organizations such as appointment of new officers, rising or falling earnings, product or service obsolescence, new regulations, and occasionally even mismanagement or fraud. The challenge is to respond carefully and positively while avoiding classic mistakes such as firing the messenger or abruptly changing a fundamentally sound strategy.

It is more difficult to deal with subtle crises because only a few trustees recognize them. In addition, those trustees themselves might not be sure that their observations are correct and worthy of committee attention, or they suspect that their points of view will not be well received by other trustees.

Subtle crises are not sudden changes; they are the evolving alterations in an economy, market, or institution that are easily recognized by hindsight but difficult to foresee. Subtle crises include increasing inflation, the aging of the population, computerization, and increasing use of fast food. Occasionally, ignoring subtle trends brings corporations and their investors to disaster's front door. One example is the effect that new highways and jet planes had on railroad industry profits. Thousands of investors failed to foresee difficulties and were left holding Penn Central Railroad commercial paper when the company defaulted in 1968. A former state political leader described another example as follows:

During the gasoline shortages of the 1970s, I met an automobile industry executive and told him I thought American manufacturers should produce more small cars like the Germans and Japanese. "Don't worry," he said. "Americans have a permanent love affair with large cars and we will build them. When gasoline supplies increase Americans will go back to big cars." Such was the genesis of American automobile industry competitive decline and financial strain.

A final example is the inability of utility industry executives (and their governmental supporters) to evaluate correctly anti-nuclear protests and the effects of both inflation and increasing regulatory costs on nuclear plant construction. The result was huge financial losses as nuclear plants were left unfinished.

In portfolio management, introduction of investment securities (standardized option contracts, financial futures contracts, collateralized mortgage obligations, and others), as well as passage of the Employee Retirement Income Security Act (ERISA) in 1974 and the Tax Reform Act of 1986, produced important changes not well understood at the time. Other examples are the use of low-rated securities to finance corporate mergers and acquisitions, and protest movements such as the drive for socially responsible investing. These trends have been important. They have offered opportunity; they have had risk. But at their inception, it was difficult to measure their significance. It was especially challenging to avoid loss in junk bonds and extra transaction costs to eliminate socially unacceptable securities.

Assuredly, boards and investment committees that discuss both obvious and subtle crises early in their evolution produce better results for plan sponsors, but there are practical forces that delay or misdirect these discussions. Some are 10-year memories, impatience, comparing inappropriately personal to institutional results, failure to plan and to organize for crises and to keep detailed records and minutes, and inadequate use of consultants.

TEN-YEAR MEMORIES

We think in decades. It was the "roaring 20s," "the fabulous 50s" and "the tumultuous 60s," as if life proceeds in 10-year blocks. Investment reporting services think this way, and their numerous charts on stocks, mutual funds, and the market comprise 10-year periods. Accordingly, charts in today's periodicals do not cover events more than 10 years old.

The importance of visible data (10-year charts) compared to invisible data (occurrences more than 10 years old) rests in our propensity to predict that what is happening now will continue to occur. If it is raining this morning, we say, "It will be a rainy day." According to an investment newsletter, this predilection influences investment decisions because "at any given time the mood of investors (and the public at large) is conditioned primarily by the events of immediately preceding years."[1]

There is no better representation of this tendency than a famous cover story in *Business Week* titled "The Death of Equities." It said, "Today, the old idea of buying solid stocks as a cornerstone for one's life savings and retirement has simply disappeared."[2] At this time (late 1970s) it was an unembarrassed assertion because the stock market had done poorly for almost 10 years. Nevertheless, like the newspaper headline "Dewey Wins," it was wrong, for the second greatest bull market in modern history started in August 1982, and investors who followed *Business Week's* implied advice missed a great opportunity. They were reacting to results of recent years and were not sensitive to the potential proved by great markets in the 60s and early 70s—more than 10 years earlier.

Conversely, there is a penchant to commit too much capital *after* markets have appreciated. This is an almost irresistible compulsion to think that an asset or a market that appreciated 10 percent last month will appreciate 10 percent next month. The compulsion was especially apparent during the early months of 1987 when thousands of investors bought stocks as averages rose to highs—just before the October decline—because they had forgotten the risks (taught by the bear market of 1973–74) that no longer appeared on 10-year charts.

IMPATIENCE

We want results right now! Unfortunately, a market operates on its agenda, not ours. Forgive the alliteration, but patience, persistence, and perspective produce profit.

PERSONAL EXPERIENCES

The taxpayer is to governmental finance what the individual investor is to an institutional investment account. Private experiences with personal budgets or investment portfolios alone do not inculcate a comprehensive perception. The following are examples:

- A trustee whose own company stock is declining is likely to fear the whole market.
- An individual who has purchased specific stocks or mutual funds believes that those securities are appropriate for a larger organization.
- A speculator who has lost money in commodities rejects the hedging potential inherent in option and futures contracts.
- Individuals resist acquiring long-term bonds for their institution because they will not buy them for themselves.
- A trustee who recently had good results from a mutual fund of low-rated debt securities feels comfortable recommending them to his institution, but another trustee rejects the proposal because he had a bad experience.[3]

PLANNING

The Federal Reserve Board of the United States has a written action plan for crisis management. It apparently describes how the chairperson should act personally to avoid exacerbating the crisis, who should talk to whom, how to relate to foreign governments, and how to deal with the media.

Every investment committee will experience an obvious crisis. There should be a plan to deal with it.

Every investment committee will experience subtle crisis. Long-range planning subcommittees and open brainstorming meetings will reveal them and bring forth appropriate responses. Creation of planning subcommittees also activates trustees; it gives them an opportunity to create and to enjoy investing. Subcommittees could answer questions like these:

- How would we respond to inflation? Deflation?
- What are the 10 most powerful economic trends in the United States today? Do they mean opportunities for us?
- What should be the style of our next money manager?
- What opportunities exist in other markets of the world?
- How can we improve trustee training?
- Is our own committee organization effective and efficient? What do recent studies on governance suggest?

WRITTEN RECORDS

A straitjacket of ignorance enslaves trustees when it is impossible for them to read a history of their organization. How can a trustee vote to change a strategy if there is no written record of why it was adopted?

Keep records, including dissenting points of view. Insert them in the minutes. Require new trustees to read them.

CONSULTANTS

Everyone has a consultant, the person who gets things done. For individuals investing jointly, the consultant is the one who calls the stockbroker. For institutions, the consultant is the person who plans and organizes meetings, converses with professionals, and provides agendas and reports. The consultant might be one trustee on the committee, or a staff member, or a paid professional. Consultants are important in both routine and crisis investment management if they are sincere students of both investment theory and practical decision making. Professionals are especially effective because they observe deliberations of many different investors, investment firms, and investment committees; they have an intuitive appreciation of what works.

On the other hand, professional consultants enter into precarious marriages, and their incomes depend on avoidance of divorce. Some trustees respect consultants, but others wonder if they are worth the money. Money managers are especially skeptical about consultants, believing that consultants earn fees only by searching for new money managers, that is, by replacing or reducing the influence of current ones.

In all relationships, the individual who feels that his or her ideas are both useful and respected brings great enthusiasm, dedication, and loyalty to the client. It is the committee's responsibility to earn these benefits by clearly placing confidence in the consultant.

SUGGESTIONS

A written policy for dealing with obvious crises might read as follows: "When delay would damage potential investment returns, the chairperson or vice chairperson of the investment committee and two additional members may make binding decisions. Circumstances include unexpected receipt of a substantial gift, incapacity of a money manager, or significant changes in investment markets. If members are considering an asset allocation change in response to a significant market change, before deciding they must consult with individuals who have studied or experienced similar changes in the past."

These suggestions will help to deal with subtle crises:

1. Appoint a subcommittee to imagine what investing will be like in 10 years; contemplate potential new types and categories of securities, future uses of computers, the role of government and regulation, possible political or social movements like the trend toward socially responsible investing, future needs of beneficiaries such as retiring employees or endowment grantees, and other social phenomena that could affect investment policy.

2. Maintain a long-range planning subcommittee; create lists of acceptable new money managers should the need arise; study investment techniques like managed futures and venture capital; and decide at what point these techniques should be tried.

3. Ask three trustees to study literature: Give one trustee subscriptions to important periodicals such as the *Financial Analysts Journal,* the *Journal of Financial Planning,* and several others; give the second trustee books and audiotapes about investment practices; and give the third trustee books about organization governance. Devote a portion of each committee meeting to reports from these trustees and share the best ideas with the parent board.

4. Invite presentations by "experts" who either criticize investment practices or market trends, or who propose new techniques;

to reduce or eliminate the expense of these presentations, utilize telephone conferencing through "squawk boxes" in the meeting room.

5. Once every two years, devote up to three hours for trustees (as well as staff and consultants) to share personal ideas about the fund, their roles, their feelings and opinions, and other personal matters affecting conduct of meetings.

6. Once every five years, invite all participants in the investment process to a weekend retreat to consider all aspects of modern investment practices.

*   *   *   *   *

A maxim of motivational speakers is "Success is where the path of opportunity meets the path of preparation." Every obvious crisis contains opportunities for the well-prepared investment committee. Every subtle crisis (the trend that is just out of sight) represents either an investment opportunity or a risk to be avoided, but early detection is possible only for investment committees organized to find them. Preparation and planning make the difference. They are vitamins of long-range success.

NOTES

1. Bradlee H. Perry, *The Babson Staff Letter,* Friday, August 21, 1992, p. 1.
2. Quoted in ibid., p. 4.
3. Between 1982 and 1992, some individuals earned good returns on junk bonds while others experienced losses. Results varied with the dates of purchases and sales.

CHAPTER 14

CONFIDENTIALITY IN MAKING INVESTMENT DECISIONS

Secret: done, made, or conducted without the knowledge of others; kept from the knowledge of any but the initiated or privileged

Random House Dictionary of the English Language, 2nd ed.

A person who has information does not feel he owns a secret. If he knows it, how can it be a secret? He is flabbergasted when someone suggests that he or his committee is secretive. Nevertheless, most investing is conducted in secret.

Individuals always have guarded their personal financial affairs. They believe that governments, competitors, or even neighbors potentially could damage either their financial condition or their reputation by misuse of personal data. The strongest threat has been the tax collector, from whom, even today, millions around the world withhold important information.

Financial institutions have accommodated privacy for centuries, giving rise to an image of a trust officer or personal banker as a person of confidence, the one individual who keeps secrets. The star of this movie has been the Swiss banker and bank account, symbols of confidentiality in all kinds of adventures.

There also has been mystery around charismatic men of finance such as Bernard Baruch, Joseph Kennedy, and Jesse Livermore, or more recently Jerry Tsai, Warren Buffett, Peter Lynch, and John Templeton. Early in the century, such men were believed to have both talent and inside (secret) information. In recent years, great investing has been attributed to talent because laws both prevent the use of inside information and promote the dissemination of important data.

The tradition of personal privacy in "high finance" has fostered the confidentiality prevalent today. Thousands of investment committees keep decisions private. They effectively withhold information by observing three customs: failing to keep records, limiting distribution, and making quiet appointments.

Failing to keep records is not limited to investment committees. Most groups do not keep adequate records, and frequently it is impossible to determine who attended a meeting, who proposed and seconded motions, which trustees supported and opposed a motion, and how many voted for or against. Instead, formal minutes state only, "It was agreed to hire an investment manager," or a similar generality, which gives readers no clue about the history or debate behind the decision. Records fail to outline how committees formulated the original list of potential money managers, what each manager said during interviews, and why they selected specific managers. Committees also do not chronicle points of view of individual trustees, ideas presented by consultants, why policies were adopted and who prepared drafts, prices proposed by different competitors, and countless other details that permit future trustees to comprehend past decisions. Facts and conclusions not recorded cannot be disseminated. They remain secrets by default.

Limiting distribution, the second custom supporting confidentiality, means failing to publish decisions in periodicals. Newsletters and annual reports of both companies and nonprofits seldom report anything about the organization's investments. The only way a customer, constituent, supporter, beneficiary, or employee can learn about investment activities is to request information directly. It is embarrassing to do this because sources tend to ask, "Why do you want it?" Also, if the information is available at all in convenient written form, staff members do not believe they are authorized to provide it.

The most powerful phenomenon encouraging secrecy is making quiet appointments: withholding names of individuals responsible for investment policy. Annual reports, directories, and newsletters do not list names, addresses, or telephone numbers of investment committee trustees. Also, national directories customarily list only a "contact person," such as a controller, who frequently is unauthorized or unwilling to give out information. The result: Only the involved, or the most interested and aggressive outsiders, know what is going on.

Confidentiality does have benefits. Social activists, for example, cannot protest policies and decisions of which they are unaware. While trustees tend to view most investment decisions dispassionately, an investment affecting less than $1/10$ of 1 percent of a portfolio can set off well-organized protests if beneficiaries or supporters believe that the investment offends their ethical standards. (Students protest investments in South Africa, religious groups oppose companies that manufacture cigarettes and alcohol, and retirement plan employees disagree with acquisition of securities of competing companies.) Whether justified or not, rectifying the wrong is expensive and probably of no interest to most participants.

Another benefit of confidentiality is being able to avoid explaining the unexplainable. Since investing is more art than science, explaining decisions is difficult. Investment managers routinely acquire unknown or *speculative* securities to *reduce portfolio risk,* an incomprehensible contradiction to lay observers. Trustees themselves allocate assets to unusual investment categories such as portfolio insurance programs or managed futures, decisions that would require reams of paper to explain. It is especially difficult to spell out why one money management firm was hired instead of another, and attempting to explain engenders confusion and hard feelings. Differences between firms are intangible, not easily described. They include style, techniques of screening and timing, attitudes like "top-down" or "contrarian,"or even sophisticated programs such as tactical or strategic asset allocation. Many trustees themselves have only minimal understanding of how one firm operates compared to another. Therefore, trustees would not welcome an obligation to explain their chores.

Personal considerations further abet passive concealment. While trustees enjoy investment activities, they also fear loss. Mighty are both the psychological and practical effects of loss. Neither an investment committee nor a trustee wants to be accountable for investment losses, and many would refuse to serve if they had to assume this risk. Public disclosure could discourage easygoing, candid discussions that foster good communication and thorough consideration of issues, especially questions of personality. Trustees make abstract judgments. Although not clairvoyant, they may be held legally responsible for decisions that don't work out. Trustees are relieved of this pressure by maintaining confidentiality, making quiet appointments, recording only final decisions, and delegating specific security selection to professional money managers. Also, if their names are unknown, trustees will not receive unsolicited sales calls from vendors of financial services.

Yet there is a case against concealment that encompasses both moral beliefs and pragmatic issues of accountability and results. The focus of any moral contention favoring disclosure and accountability is the frequently unanswerable question: "Who owns this organization?" No organization has a comprehensive answer, and some have no answer at all.

Until passage of the Employee Retirement Income Security Act (ERISA) in 1974, employee benefit plans were widely considered property of the sponsoring company. ERISA transferred "ownership" of employee benefit assets to the employees themselves, at least in principle, and subsequent laws and regulations have both ensured the value of plans and placed obligations on their trustees to avoid loss and to restrict the use of plan assets for the benefit of the company.[1] Still, some issues remain unresolved and require judgment. In small companies, retirement plans might have only one or two beneficiaries, who also are owners. It can be argued that these trustees may make unusual investment decisions because they literally are dealing with their money without significant fiduciary obligations to others. But at what number of employees does the obligation to others exceed the obligation to themselves? Five employees? Ten? One hundred? Also, many plans pay defined benefits, and if these plans earn higher rates of return than required to meet obligations, the company can reduce future contributions, thereby improving the net worth of its shares. The question "Who owns our plan?" never will be answered completely, and there always will be tension between owners/managers and employees. But to the extent it is believed that they own employee benefit plans, employee beneficiaries are morally entitled to unimpaired full disclosure about the actions of their trustees.

If it is difficult to determine who owns employee benefit plans, it is impossible to determine who owns nonprofits. Suppose a large foundation was funded by one benefactor years ago and since has become a major source of support for community activities. Is it still owned by a self-perpetuating board of trustees? Are beneficiaries such as community social action agencies entitled to influence foundation investment policy? Should there be important relationships between the foundation and its founder or the founder's company? Since "the public" provided significant estate and income tax benefits to both contributors and beneficiaries, is the public thereby entitled to influence policy or even to elect its trustees and to review financial audits?

Educational institutions present even greater dilemmas. Who truly owns a school? Trustees? Today's students? Tomorrow's students? The administration? What about alumni, individual and corporate donors, or even the elusive "public" that agreed to give up tax revenues to encourage education? In practice, there is no question of who owns college and university endowments: It is the investment committees that exercise rights of ownership by making decisions. If it is accepted that certain constituencies have vested economic interests in a school's financial health, then it is easy to make a moral argument favoring full, voluntary disclosure of those decisions. Disclosure facilitates influence; it allows constituencies to make their views known. It also empowers onlookers to evaluate results.

Because trustees appear to have done well for their institutions, moral arguments against confidentiality do not motivate governance changes. No one ever has questioned the integrity, honesty, loyalty and enthusiasm that volunteer trustees bring to their work, and observers in other nations marvel at the time and money volunteers donate to American nonprofits. Yet there remains a most interesting proposition: Investment accounts of nonprofits might do even better if they were subjected to public scrutiny.

Although data linking full disclosure to better results does not exist, intuition suggests there is a connection. Assumptions that support this suggestion include the following.

1. Sharing information accelerates opinion formation. Letters to the editor, speeches in the Senate, and debates at scientific conferences all originate from printed or broadcast information.

2. Individuals do better in public. Whether one is an athlete, a journalist, a public speaker, a writer, an investment manager, or a trustee, the motivation toward excellence is increased when one's performance is reviewed in public.

3. To compete, we must have information about competitors. This is human nature. We want to beat the previous owner of an achievement. "I want to drive faster than Mario Andretti" is a more convincing motivation to improve racing car performance than "I want to drive faster than average." A mutual fund manager is more satisfied by doing better than another specific fund or a universe of funds than by beating a popular index or average. Popular mutual fund scorecards list performance within a mutual fund category, not against broad market averages. However, trustees cannot compete in this manner because there is no public data comparing one plan sponsor to another. It is as if the Chicago Bears know only that they play football and that *on average* other teams are doing better, but they do not know the specific record of the Dallas Cowboys, their next competitor.[2] Trustees operate in this competitive vacuum; investment committees have a rough idea of how their results compare to averages and to unnamed but similar investment accounts, but they have no idea of how a specific competing institution is doing.

4. Outsiders cannot or will not offer suggestions to entities that do not welcome advice. There is no practical method that allows a friend and supporter, even an alum of a college or a beneficiary of a retirement plan, to offer suggestions if the plan sponsor operates confidentially. The supporter does not know when or where to send his or her thoughts. In such an environment, Einstein's theory of relativity never would have made it beyond his front door. (There is a cartoon frequently circulated among salespeople. It shows a king, backed by an army with bows and arrows, facing his enemy. Behind the king is a salesman offering new technology: the machine gun. The king refuses to see the salesman and says, "I don't have time for any salesman. I've got a war to fight.")

PERSONAL COMMENTARY

The comprehensive confidentiality of trustee-directed funds is impressive. It is a barrier to understanding that also has benefits. During preparation of this book, I began to see larger issues, especially when one important source denied me permission to publish its data. The experience surprised me so much that I began to think more deeply about its implications. But first, I will offer some background.

Retirement plan and nonprofit investment activities involve two major players: money managers and investment committees. (Actuaries also are important for retirement plans.) There is ample information about money managers and mutual funds because they report results to consultant-sponsored data bases, and private managers routinely mail their performance numbers to clients and prospective clients. Furthermore, the Association for Investment Management and Research (AIMR) has formulated its uniform Performance Presentation Standards, by which money managers report results. The intent is to have reliable data about the specific contributions of professional money managers.

On the other hand, there is little reliable, comparable, publicly available information about *overall* plans that trustees manage, and it is impossible to measure the results of decisions of one investment committee against those of another. Trustees are responsible for the big picture. They allocate portions of the total fund to cash and to different managers, and the result of these decisions is the total return of the entire fund. If a committee hires Growth Manager A, who does well, but also hires Small Cap Manager B, who does poorly, the total result may be mediocre. In addition, if the committee places specific restrictions on a manager (such as minimum credit ratings, maximum maturities, or so-cially responsible criteria), then it materially affects the manager's per-formance, but there is no practical way to account for these decisions. In other words, there is no way for independent, outside observers to mea-sure the contribution of trustees.

It is theoretically possible for plan sponsors to study each other. For example, nonprofits, retirement plans, and public employee benefit plans do share some data *with each other*. The medium for sharing is either an association or a consultant. Nonprofits tend to use associations whose central office solicits total return information by mailing questionnaires. Each institution responds voluntarily, and the central office publishes an annual report that compares average results of all participating institu-tions to market indexes, lists money managers hired by each, describes spending policies, and gives average turnover rates (a measure of trading activities). The report lists results of individual institutions in confidence by using a number code, which means that a board can recognize its own numbers but cannot identify others. There is weakness in the raw data because each institution answers its questionnaire independently and un-audited based on its own interpretation of the questions and its particular accounting system. Also, reported average results have a positive bias because every year a number of institutions do not respond, presumably those with the poorest performance, a phenomenon called manager-attrition bias.

Retirement plans have better data because they tend to hire master trustees (companies that process all transactions for a plan sponsor), and master trustees can report results directly to consultant-sponsored data services. It is then possible for the consultant to report how each client performed compared to all other clients. However, consultants, like as-sociations, report in confidence by using codes or dots on a graph. Therefore, it is not possible for Plan A to compare its policies and pro-cedures to those of Plan B, because neither knows the other specifically.

I have been aware of association annual reports and have occasion-ally asked acquaintances to send me copies. None has done so. While discussing this matter with a friend and colleague, I learned that he, too, had asked some of his acquaintances to send him reports, but none had done so. Then another friend/colleague told me that his association of investment executives explicitly prohibits distribution of information out-side the association.

None of this was important until I started writing this book. Obvi-ously, such data might prove or disprove various hypotheses. Therefore, with persistence, I obtained performance data from one association and used the data in the draft of one chapter. I sent the chapter to the organization for permission to publish and received the following phone call: "Mr. Guy, I have bad news. You may not publish our data."

"Why?" I asked.

"Because your premise is wrong."

Then I asked for an opportunity to discuss it further and got this response: "Our chief executive is too busy to speak to you, and additional requests will irritate him. He thinks your premise is wrong, and he has more experience than you and I combined."

This response brought to mind a related experience. A few years ago, I asked a research assistant to obtain data about a certain category of tax-exempt investment accounts. He phoned over 60 accounts, but none provided performance information or names of responsible trustees or staff. (At the time, I thought it was just sales resistance.) Finally, in preparing to write this book, I asked more than a dozen investment committees for permission to observe a meeting. None complied, and one said, "It makes us too uncomfortable."

As this book neared completion, I learned about the work of anthropologist William M. O'Barr and attorney John M. Conley for the Institutional Investor Project of the Columbia Law School. They said:

> Private [pension] funds tend to behave like private corporations in matters of communication. They view the details of their investment strategies and performance as trade secrets. Throughout our interviews, we were given pieces of information on the condition that we respect their proprietary nature (We have done so, of course.) There is little communication with other funds about these topics, even on a general level. Private funds typically subscribe to services that report the performance of all large funds, but with the names deleted. They can identify themselves and can therefore see where they rank, but they do not know how specific competitors are doing, or, more significantly, how well particular strategies are working in the pension world as a whole. The general lack of mobility of personnel from one private pension fund to another also helps limit the flow of information. As a result, private fund executives have little basis for comparing the efficacy of the various strategies among which they must choose. . . . One issue that seemed particularly sensitive at one of the public funds was whether we would be permitted to observe the portion of a trustees' meeting at which investment strategy would be discussed. After consultation between investment professionals and lawyers, we were excluded.[3]

The point is that confidentiality is important to boards of trustees and investment committees. But why is it so important, and does it make a difference? I have no way of knowing for sure, and no method to prove my hypothesis, but I think the answer may be found in the portion of human nature that is embarrassed by decisions that cannot be rationally explained. Individuals who are accustomed to managing tangibles seem self-consciousness when asked to manipulate intangibles. Most people can explain personal or business decisions in practical terms. Examples might be "I built the deck because we need a place to relax," "We designed the laptop computer for use on airplanes," or "We need a new science center to attract top students." In these examples, the needs are reasonable and the results measurable. The decision-making process is orderly and is based on visible needs fully comprehensible to an observer, and contractors are hired based on objective criteria such as skill and price.

It is not the same with investing. Our language does not have enough words to explain *exactly* why a board places 20 percent in bonds, 40 percent in growth stocks, 20 percent in small cap stocks, 10 percent in venture capital, and 10 percent in managed futures. It is simply impossible to explain these decisions to outside observers. In fact, it is embarrassing to try, because the explanations do not sound plausible even to the spokesperson. Why does a board hire Modern Portfolio Management, Inc., instead of Old-Fashioned Growth Stocks, Inc.? Both work in the same market, charge the same fees, and have access to similar information sources. Their recent performance statistics are different, but their 10-year average results are about the same. Frequently the honest explanation is that the choice "felt right." Since a journalist, an author, or even a beneficiary might not have the same feeling, it is embarrassing to have them in the room. Imagine this newspaper headline: "State Board Hires Semiduration Bond Managers, Inc., Because 'It Felt Right.' " Yet that is the most accurate explanation. When an investment committee meets, its decisions are intuitive. That's just the way it is. To avoid making long, superficial-sounding explanations, and to protect themselves from attendant embarrassment, boards seek confidentiality.

I think confidentiality is useful. Most investment committees make better decisions in private than they would in public, and many trustees would not serve under public scrutiny. Nevertheless, I lament the missing information. Without it, one board cannot compete against another, and it is not possible to prove any hypothesis about investment committee effectiveness. Therefore, we who choose to present opinions and to offer suggestions for improvement have to work with scarce information, with impressions drawn only from personal experiences. Just like the boards we study, we use intuition as our guide.

SUGGESTIONS

1. Electronically record every investment committee meeting. Transcribe or condense the recording. Publish details or announce availability. If publication is too expensive, allow interested parties to listen to the recording at the organization's office. Reproduce all final decisions in the minutes of the sponsor.
2. Publicly announce dates and times of investment committee meetings. Permit qualified interested observers to attend.
3. List the names of trustees and their committee assignments in annual reports.
4. Assign one trustee or staff member to receive, record, and acknowledge outside ideas and opinions, and to report at each committee meeting.
5. In a widely distributed periodical such as an alumni magazine, annual report, or company employee newsletter, publish (a) the investment policy; (b) the names of money managers and dollar allocation to each; (c) the total return on the entire fund for the last five years; and (d) a discussion about how results were achieved, how they compare to indexes, and (if possible) how they compare to results of similar institutions and why they vary from those institutions.
6. Place a Welcome sign over the door by entertaining new ideas from any source.

NOTES

1. Neither this paragraph nor any other information in this book provides advice about legal and regulatory compliance. This book focuses exclusively on plan governance and the effects of practices such as confidentiality.

2. There is good data comparing one money manager to another, but none comparing the work of one named investment committee to another named investment committee.
3. William M. O'Barr and John M. Conley, *Fortune & Folly: The Wealth & Power of Institutional Investing* (Homewood, Ill.: Business One Irwin, 1992), pp. 137–38.

CHAPTER 15

TRAINING TRUSTEES

Training is everything. The peach was once a bitter almond; cauliflower is nothing but cabbage with a college education.

Mark Twain

Trustees must acquire *money sense*. What is money sense? The answer is elusive, like the definition of an artist or a world leader. Money sense is an intangible multifaceted understanding of the dynamics of capital.

One important component of money sense is *urgency,* a perspective on the time value of money that produces in the investor a strong need to make decisions expeditiously—to get the job done—because delay negatively affects rates of return. Therefore, a trustee who has money sense is likely to press for efficient governance, a decision-making system that operates quickly and is prepared for most contingencies.

Money sense also insists on understanding *compound interest,* that marvelous, powerful process that enhances wealth, facilitates comfortable retirements, beats inflation, and helps to build great endowments. According to a popular tale, physicist Albert Einstein was asked, ''Sir, what is the greatest invention in history?'' His answer: ''Compound interest, of course!''

A quick way to evaluate effects of compound interest is the Rule of 72. To learn how long it takes money to double, divide a compound interest rate into 72. If the rate is 10 percent, $1,000 will become $2,000 in 7.2 years; at 15 percent, 4.8 years; at 4 percent, over 18 years for the sum to double. The rewards of seeking higher returns, and allowing continuous reinvestment of both accumulated income and capital gains, increase over time. The Rule of 72 also indicates the critical role of spending policies, because earnings spent cannot compound. Furthermore, allowing money to compound is the source of satisfaction in personal periodic savings and investment programs. Those who have confidence in compound interest feel urgency as they begin to understand the overpowering value of time.

Time sense is another useful tool for trustees. A perspective on time is both simple and complex. At its most elementary, time sense is knowing what day it is, when the next appointment is, how long it takes to get from one place to another, and what one's position is in the scale of young to old. We all know individuals who lack these faculties (e.g., those who never arrive on time). More relevant are investors who manage personal assets around time-related premises such as "I am too old to invest" or "If I lose money, there is not enough time for me to earn back the amount lost." These premises are myths acquired without investigation, but thousands of individuals—from ages 35–85—base decisions on them every year.

Physicists articulate the most complex views of time because they are concerned with an expanding universe and distances measured in light years. Fortunately, trustees do not have to acknowledge the physicist's eternity, but they do have to visualize a responsibility to future beneficiaries. A college, for example, probably has an infinite life span, and decisions by trustees today profoundly affect future capabilities to serve. In this context, time sense and money sense are inextricably linked to investment decisions because investment committee trustees should imagine benefits to students gathered around electric cars and watch-size computers 20, 30, or even 100 years from now. Decisions today affect benefits far in the future.

There also is an important connection between time and value. Trustees need a *sense of value*, a conception of how today's prices, price-earnings ratios, interest rates, and dividend yields compare to similar values of the past. It is the only way to know if something is high or low. An investor without this aspect of time and money sense is likely to be dogmatic. He or she might immodestly believe that interest rates must rise. "They have no other way to go," the investor states, without even acknowledging the possibility of decline. The reason for such certainty is lack of knowledge about deflationary periods like the Great Depression. Simply put, trustees must learn market history, a necessary building block toward a sense of time and value.

With a solid background in market history, trustees are likely to begin making an effective distinction between yesterday and tomorrow. The ability to *separate past and future* must be real, not intellectual. Every investor can comfortably verbalize that what happened yesterday might not happen today or tomorrow, but many investors reveal through action that they really do not believe it. One revealing action is selling a stock "because it has not done well the last six months," or buying a stock after it has risen significantly because "it is bound to be a good investment." These investors presume a significant extension of trends recently perceived. Thousands of investors act on such presumptions, thereby creating heavy trading volume near the top of bull markets and low volume near the bottom of bear markets. Investors alternate between euphoria and pessimism depending on *recent* trends that might or might not continue. Institutions demonstrate the same tendency by firing money managers who have not done well *recently* and hiring those *recently* reporting above-average results.

Interpreters of investment history and theory present an interesting challenge to those learning money sense. First, they ask trustees to resist making decisions based only on recent results such as price trends. At the same time, however, risk calculations such as beta, range, and standard deviation depend for their credibility on faith in both recent and long-term data. It is difficult to reject one use of data (acting on recent results) and to accept another (using recent data to calculate risk), but trustees with time sense and money sense can do it.

Meanwhile, investors with money sense focus on the *big picture*. They believe in portfolios instead of products. What counts in their eyes is the totality of an entire investment program instead of its components. In contrast, individual investors managing personal portfolios have an observable tendency to purchase or sell a single asset, such as one stock, without awareness of their entire personal financial condition. Investor A, for example, follows 10 stocks every day and earns 8 percent to 15 percent per year on his stock portfolio, but he also maintains a large checking account that earns no interest at all. The result is mediocre total return. Meanwhile, investor B is so proud of 2 of his 15 stocks that he fails to notice a serious decline in another that reduces total return to average. These investors lack money sense. They are students of products such as stocks or bonds instead of the entire package of financial assets that make up their net worths.

The final and most important component of comprehensive money sense is *personal acceptance of risk*. Acceptance is an intense awareness, greater than indicated by the common statement "There is risk in everything." It is a capacity to assume that things *normally* go wrong, usually coupled with confidence that humans can set them right. The following examples demonstrate normal risk:

1. Insurance companies budget for all kinds of risks based on experience. The risks include violent hurricanes and other tragedies

that appear abnormal when they occur but that are statistically normal occurrences.

2. It is normal for a company to experience crises caused by product obsolescence, manufacturing difficulties, and organizational stress. Securities analysts believe that every company, especially every rapidly growing enterprise, suffers setbacks. No company grows at an uninterrupted, steady pace. Therefore, investors do not need to ask whether a crisis will occur, because it will. Instead, the questions are When? and Does the company have both financial resources and management skills to handle it? If risk is viewed this way, trustees and their advisors can consider negative company news as a normal phenomenon to be rationally considered instead of an emergency requiring rapid surgery.

3. Political change is normal. In just over 200 years, our nation has had more than 40 presidents. Hence, it may be an exaggeration to predict that the economy or stock market will suffer or benefit just because so-and-so is elected.

4. At least since the days of the Dutch West India Company, prices of intangible securities have gone both up and down. Therefore, it is normal for markets to move down and for investors to suffer occasional declines in net worth. Trustees who dispassionately accept declines as normal can evaluate them effectively. (Trustees also must correctly evaluate probabilities of appreciation. Lecturers ask audiences, "Is it reasonable to expect $10 stocks to rise to $15 in six months?" About half the audience responds affirmatively, bespeaking lack of money sense. The expectation, in general, is unattainable and unreasonable.)

Trustees may study two categories of investment risk: systematic and unsystematic. The first category includes the inescapable perils of an entire environment, such as the stock market as a whole. The second covers risks attributable to one element in that environment, such as a single stock. A single company can experience negative results (unsystematic risk) while the market and economy (the entire "system") are doing well. Trustees with money sense appreciate the difference between these two categories as well as the range of possibilities. Both a company and the market can do well simultaneously, or they do poorly at the same time. Fortunately, theorists have proved that trustees can eliminate unsystematic risk—if they want to. By purchasing enough securities from different segments of the market, and controlling relative weightings of each, an investment program will have only systematic risk. Of course, if trustees want to concentrate funds, in effect assuming unsystematic risk, they may do so.

To teach both money sense and the general responsibilities of board members/trustees, groups must train constantly. Cyrill O. Houle put it this way:

> The importance of an effective orientation to a board for either novice or veteran trustees probably does not need to be stressed, nor are the possible techniques obscure. As an experienced board chairman once remarked, "Everybody really knows what to do; they just don't take the time to do it."[1]

SUGGESTIONS FOR TRAINING NEW TRUSTEES

Adapting Houle's ideas to investment committees produces the following suggestions:

1. Adopt a training goal—creation of money sense—and formulate a plan to achieve it.
2. Assign an experienced trustee to direct new trustee education.
3. Designate one experienced investment committee trustee to "sponsor" each new member to ensure that the new member has all of the necessary information and that all personal introductions have been made.
4. Give a specific task to each new committee member. Possible assignments include maintaining a permanent record of committee debates and decisions; developing a committee library of books, periodicals, and audiotapes and circulating them among members; developing and maintaining a list of acceptable money managers to contact at once should a need arise; providing a monthly synopsis of important published investment commentaries to other trustees; purchasing new books on investing and asking other trustees to read and review them in writing; and researching and commenting on new investing techniques and new investment securities such as managed futures, venture capital, international markets, collateralized mortgage obligations,

exchangeable preferred stocks, adjustable and floating rate issues, and wrap fee accounts.

5. Hold a special meeting to orient new committee members. The agenda could include:
   a. History of the organization and its investment policy. Copies of the minutes and other documents recording investment decisions should be provided.
   b. Presentation of the investment policy and discussion about the theories on which it is based.
   c. Presentation of the spending policy and either the actuarial or budgetary assumptions used to create it.
   d. Personal talks by the consultant and one or two of the investment managers about how they see their functions. If necessary, this could be done through a telephone "squawk box" (also known as a "shout down").
   e. An open conversation about what is expected of trustees (reading, attending meetings, handling assigned tasks, etc.).

6. Ask a new member to act as liaison with one of the committee's money managers and to report in writing both the manager's results and current strategy; assign one committee member, new or experienced, to each money manager and to the consultant for the same purposes.

7. Acquire a membership for a new trustee in an association of professional investors, and ask him or her to report on the association's work.

SUGGESTIONS FOR CONTINUING EDUCATION OF ALL TRUSTEES

1. Profit from the knowledge and skills of professional advisors. At every meeting, the consultant and the money managers should teach something, explain a concept, provide a new idea, or outline an economic theory or market scenario. Professionals are the most talented investors in the world, and trustees should extract their best ideas. (Usually, investment professionals assume that personal meetings are for reporting results, explaining investment philosophies, and continuing good relationships, i.e., keeping the account. They are reluctant to stray outside

the traditional limits of investment presentations. Committees, therefore, must solicit new ideas in an atmosphere of confidence and respect while demonstrating that the goals are merely to share and to brainstorm.)

2. Send at least two trustees, or a trustee and staff member, to one of the public presentations frequently offered by periodicals, associations, investment consultants, and educational institutions. Make it clear that those who attend must render a written report about their experience.

3. Appoint as investment committee chair an individual who is truly interested in investment techniques and trustee training, and who has the time, inclination, and administrative skills to do the job.

> (The chairperson) must be aware of the need for developing the abilities of board members more rapidly than by letting nature take its course. In doing so, she must be subtle, for her role is not defined as that of a teacher, and, in fact, she is really more of a fellow student—even though, for a time, first among equals—than an instructor. She should remember Alexander Pope's maxim:
>
> Men must be taught as if you taught them not,
> And things unknown proposed as things forgot.[2]

The board of directors should immediately replace any chairperson, no matter how prominent or apparently qualified, who does not share, delegate, communicate, and train, for the future costs of trustee ignorance are staggering.

4. Every issue must be discussed in full. No debate should be cut short. Two hypotheses of administration amplify this principle. The first states that the worst products and services were agreed to unanimously. The second is that there *always* is a reason for not doing something. If that reason is not revealed in debate, the organization is embarking on dangerous territory. Furthermore, full discussion is a training technique.

5. Every 24 months, consider changes in committee governance. Ask, "Are we as trustees effectively administering our fund?" This discussion will be educational for everyone.

6. Assign trustees to share information with other, similar institutions. For example, an investment committee trustee from one college could be invited to sit in on committee meetings of another. Investment trustees who are volunteers seldom meet and interact one-on-one with peers at other institutions. Although most institutions such as colleges, museums, and retirement plans are affiliated with peer group associations that hold annual investment conferences, the majority of conference

participants are professionals like executive directors, treasurers, and controllers. Consequently, responsible volunteers do not acquire solid relationships and good communications with their peers at other institutions. The solution is to promote cooperation and information sharing both among similar institutions and across institutional categories. There could be relationships between boards of a large and a small retirement plan, a large retirement plan and an endowment, a university endowment and a small college endowment, a museum in one city and a museum in another, the scholarship fund of a college and the benefit fund of a national fraternity or sorority. These direct relationships could be made to flourish merely by asking someone to promote them.

*   *   *   *   *

It is crucial to carry out these and other methods of educating trustees. As Houle has said, "A collective duty . . . exists. The institution's ability to achieve its mission is hampered by ignorance or apathy on the part of its trustees, and therefore the whole board has the obligation to stimulate, guide, and assist each of its members."[3]

Trustee training programs must advance two levels of money sense. Individuals must have money sense. Committees also must have money sense. A committee's money sense is not the sum of its members' money sense. It is a unique sensitivity born of members' ideas, motivated by the institutional setting and modified by compromise.

Individuals acquire money sense independently through managing personal assets, listening, and reading. Their personal competence, as well as pleasure and satisfaction, is increased by their conscious, disciplined effort to read and to attend educational meetings. This has to be a self-designed and internally motivated curriculum appropriate to the particular temperament of each trustee.

Meanwhile, all trustees on an investment committee also must seek a common money sense derived from both conscious programming and informal sharing. The investment committee must evaluate both facts and philosophies—and it must understand the difference between them. The "famous" archaeologist/philosopher Indiana Jones made this point with respect to science by saying, "Archaeology is the search for fact, not truth. If it is truth you're interested in, Dr. Tyres' philosophy class is right down the hall."[4]

Investment truths are philosophical, subject to healthy skepticism, and changeable. It has been said, "Every time I figure out how to make money in the market, they change the rules." Knowing that investment principles have changed and will continue to change is part of the committee money sense that can be acquired through continuous education. Fortunately, modern portfolio theory gives trustees a fine conceptual framework within which to begin the hunt. Its attention to the interaction among asset classes over time, based on computer capabilities both to obtain and to massage more than seven decades of data, can be the basis of a training program. Trustees also can examine theories that existed before modern portfolio theory, and they can learn to expect new and important theories in the future. Committees and individuals can build money sense if they just take the time to do it.

NOTES

1. Cyril O. Houle, *Governing Boards: Their Nature and Nurture,* (San Francisco: Jossey-Bass, 1989), p. 47.
2. Ibid., p. 51.
3. Ibid., p. 51.
4. *Indiana Jones and the Last Crusade,* Paramount Pictures, 1989.

CHAPTER 16

STAYING INFORMED

Read every day something no one else is reading. Think every day something no one else is thinking. It is bad for the mind to be always a part of a unanimity.

Christopher Morley

Four stories demonstrate that trustees should read *original* information:

- Ten people stand on stage. The first tells a joke to the second, who tells it to the third, who passes it to the fourth, and so on through the 10th person, who tells it to the audience. The audience giggles, then laughs uproariously when person one tells the *original* joke. It is not the same, and the first was best.

- George is irate. He tells Bill a political party platform unequivocally supports a social cause he dislikes. "How do you know?" asks Bill. "Senator United said so today in a letter to the editor," replies George. Bill then requests the *original* platform and learns it does support the social cause, but with important caveats that would make it more acceptable to George.

- A famous investor describes a youthful experience: "I was told that John Insidersmith was buying shares of Quickprofit Computers, Inc., so I bought some myself, but the stock declined $10 in two months. I could not understand how John could make such a mistake, so I called him. 'John,' I said. 'How could you buy Quickprofit? It never made any sense, and I don't see how you could have made such a mistake!' John responded: 'What are you talking about? I never bought Quickprofit. Why didn't you ask me first?' "[1]

- A respected brokerage firm discouraged investments in another nation. "The price-earnings ratios are too high," it said, "and there is no liquidity." Believing the best time to purchase anything is when no one else wants it, a wealthy investor visited the nation and immediately learned two things. First, the price-earnings ratios were low, but appeared high to investors unfamiliar with the nation's peculiar accounting system. He also found that liquidity appeared limited because 80 percent of transactions took place away from the national exchange. In truth, the nation had very efficient, liquid securities markets. He learned this by *original* research.

Columbus looked and found a round world; Galileo spiked a myth by dropping two objects from a leaning tower; Copernicus challenged the notion that everything revolves around the Earth, and every day investors earn greater returns by accumulating and correctly interpreting facts.

The primary obstacle to understanding is our longings. We believed the Earth was the solar system's center because we wanted humankind to be the focal point of relationships. We wanted to cure all maladies, so we believed in medicine dances and Billy Goodshape's All-Purpose Elixir. We loved railroads. They were romantic, powerful, and exciting; and they were the most important transportation for over 150 years. Therefore, we lent them money only days before bankruptcy and financial decline.[2] We want to believe humans can predict, so we pay speakers, writers, economists, and experts of every kind to tell us the economy will improve or decline, so-and-so will be elected, or the stock market will crash, advance, turn around, sell off, top out, rotate, moderate, accelerate, lead, lag, pause, or change in another way described by an intriguing verb.

We know that no one can predict accurately, but we want to believe in a predictable future. We want it so badly that we buy books and periodicals—secondary sources of data and opinion—that audaciously prognosticate. Our American, capitalistic, entrepreneurial, Old West competitive character makes us want to believe it is possible to beat the market, to earn returns that are better than both real economic growth and total average returns of stock and bond markets. Since we crave this possibility, we resist reading data that implies its impossibility. As Aristotle said, a likely impossibility is always preferable to an unconvincing possibility.

The propensity to embrace conventional ideas leads us to read conventional sources. But these sources do not contain original information. The mass circulation press, including daily business newspapers, provides news from second, third, or fourth parties. When news breaks, an official observes and interprets what happened. Then he or she tells a reporter, who discusses it with other observers and editors before preparing a story millions read. A radio announcer broadcasts an abbreviated version every half hour. Readers and listeners pass it to their friends and associates with modifications born of incomplete memories. Ergo, by the time news reaches you and me, it has been modified, exaggerated, edited, interpreted, and biased by innumerable eyes and ears.[3]

Of greater significance to trustees is information not published at all. Editors publish news they think is important to large numbers of readers. This is logical, and inevitable, because the most powerful resolve of any institution is self-preservation, the requisite need to maintain itself, to grow, and to attract viewers or readers. A distribution system must package information attractively with eye-popping, plausible headlines, for on this survival depends. Innovation, creation, and the colorless wisdom of portfolio management never make the front page. The *Daily Vienna* (and most of the world) hardly noticed Mozart's life and death. Enduring movies like *It's a Wonderful Life* and *The Wizard of Oz* initially were not successful. Gene Roddenberry's long-lived television series "Star Trek" was canceled by its first network. And the Nobel Prize Committee recognized modern portfolio theory, the greatest work of investment economics, almost 30 years after it was first developed. These staples of modern cultural and business life were too new, too far out, too complicated. They did not engage. On the other hand, the magazine cover story "Death of Equities" (*Business Week,* August 13, 1979, Dow Jones Industrial Average approximately 840) attracted readers who considered it credible because market prices had been declining. Only the well informed, the students of original information, saw through the headline.

Despite media bias toward the conventional, investment committee members must uncover facts and understand theories. To achieve maximum advantage, they have to be there first by actively pursuing primary information. They may apply the principle of original sources in two ways. First, it is a standard for evaluating competence in analysts, portfolio managers, and their investment organizations. Second, it is a guide for personal reading.

A securities analyst seeks information about industries, stocks, and bonds. He or she kicks tires and looks at the chassis and transmission. One described his work this way:

> I read *The Wall Street Journal,* but mainly I read trade journals, technical manuals and journals that evaluate products. Also, I talk to management in person. I want to talk to the chief executive, hopefully with other managers present, so I can both obtain facts and observe personal relationships. I need original information, and I need it first.[5]

THE POPULAR PRESS

Should trustees read the popular press? Of course—but with several grains of salt, because lead stories can mislead.

According to respected stock market analyst Ned Davis, newsmagazine cover stories reflect the psychology of extremes, and he suggests that the appearance of an extremely positive or extremely negative cover story illustrates popular attitudes that produce either relatively low or relatively high prices. Here is what he says:

> Paul Montgomery, a friend of mine and a very astute analyst, has studied *Time* covers since the 1920s. He found that for about 30 days after a bullish or bearish *Time* cover, the market's performance was usually consistent with the cover. In fact, if you had invested in the stock market (as suggested by the periodical) for the 30-day period following the cover stories, your investment would have gained at a rate of about 30% per annum, thus showing that cover stories have tended to occur near points of maximum momentum on the upside or downside. . . . But while the covers have been right for 30 days, he found that they have been wrong over the subsequent 11-month periods more than 80% of the time.[4]

Ned lists over 35 covers from different popular newsmagazines, each presenting a strongly positive or dramatically negative perspective, that were wrong in the long run. His conclusion: "It pays to be contrary," because major news stories appear not as a prediction of things to come, but as a reflection of ideas shared by readers. They echo an extremely popular point of view, the psychological enthusiasm or dejection at points of highest and lowest prices.

There are two ways to use this "cover story indicator." The first (appropriate only for individuals) is to trade against a story. If the story suggests bright things ahead, it is a time to be cautious, but if the story implies a dismal future, it may be time to buy. This approach to investing is called *contrarian*. For trustees, however, there is a much broader and more important lesson: A fiduciary who reads only mass circulation dailies and weeklies is likely to acquire a short-term perspective that is not useful to the institution he or she serves.

Peter Lynch said almost the same thing:

> I can't imagine anything that's useful to know that the amateur investor can't find out. All the pertinent facts are just waiting to be picked up. It didn't use to be that way, but it is now. These days, companies are required to tell nearly all in their prospectuses, their quarterlies, and their annual reports. Industry trade associations report on the general industry outlook in their publications.[6]

For the skilled explorer seeking specific new investment ideas, original research is water, fire, and air combined. To achieve superior results, trustees must assure themselves that their investment advisory organizations employ individuals who study original sources.

Trustees, however, usually meet personally only with portfolio managers—the orchestra conductors who draw on talents of analysts to place assets in logical combinations. Hence, portfolio managers must know money management theories, from conservative to radical, from accepted to outlandish. They must read the theoretical and mathematical. They must study cycles and waves, betas and standard deviations, risk and reward. Like analysts, they must create competence through their reading habits. They are perpetual students of the business scene. Just as patients want physicians who keep current, trustees want to retain well-informed investment professionals. It is tempting to suggest that trustees should hire managers based only on the question "What have you read lately?"

While trustees can judge advisors by the standard of original sources, they also should establish reading disciplines for themselves. This is not easy. Trustees are volunteers. They must read in their fields. At workday's end, it is difficult to turn mental toggle switches to unfamiliar material.

Yet it has to happen. Trustees must discern impossibilities by reading original sources and firsthand theories. They need to test theories against facts and to measure both facts and theories against personal standards of plausibility and feasibility.

Fortunately, reading for profit is fun. It's as good as seeing a movie, play, or sporting event. Strategies, intrigues, mysteries, gossip, charts, tables, graphs, hypotheses, successes, failures, humor—they're all in the fabulous literature of investing.

Why not start with a good biography, maybe of Bernard Baruch or Benjamin Graham? Then move to an opinion or system, someone's description of a sure way to get rich. Now go back to a serious work like a college text explaining portfolio theories. But be careful: Texts are tedious. Take them in small bites. Next, look for sources used in the text and read one or two. Sorry. Original sources usually are difficult. For relief, keep handy a book about a Wall Street debacle, but don't take it seriously. Read it for fun because your investment committee probably never will experience similar misadventures. Finally, be sure to peruse short stories from the investment business. These are collections of columns by insightful journalists such as Gerald Loeb, essays by respected investors such as Warren Buffett, or selections by editors such as Charles Ellis.

A trip through the land of business books is incomplete without rest stops at professional newsstands, because important ideas first appear in periodicals! Some trustees will enjoy the trade manuals and journals of the securities analyst, but it is more important to read literature aimed at portfolio managers. Take a look, for example, at the *Financial Analysts Journal,* published by the Association for Investment Management and Research, as well as university-sponsored journals like the *Harvard Business Review.*

What about a daily newspaper? Take it or leave it, but try this for variety: Subscribe to a business journal or business magazine of a distant city. These report local opinions and news found nowhere else, and their unique perspectives on national issues will illuminate, amplify, and challenge personal preconceptions. They also have regular columns about local investment markets and stocks or bonds issued by companies in their territory.

SUGGESTIONS FOR A READING PROGRAM

> We shoulda; we coulda; we wanted ta, but we didn't and we won't.
>
> *Comment by chairperson when asked about investment committee's*
> *reading program*

Advice does not always generate consent. Trustees know they should read, but it is tough to start. The following suggestions will help:

1. Appoint one person to create and administer a reading program.
2. Organize a neighborhood business-book club among trustees living near one another. Discuss one book each month.
3. Ask the consultant to recommend one new book each month. Assign a trustee to review it in writing.
4. Give each trustee a business or investment journal subscription. Ask for written summaries of relevant articles.
5. Call a portfolio manager to ask, "What is the most important book or article you have read in the last six months?" Circulate it to the committee.

6. Purchase audiotapes of professional presentations at regional and national meetings of professional investors. Listen to them in automobiles.

7. Once a year, gather committee members for lunch to discuss articles in professional and trade journals. Ask the consultant to explain complicated new concepts or mathematical models found in the journals.

8. Utilizing telephone speaker boxes, interview authors of recent articles. (In addition, committees can telephonically interview portfolio managers about new ideas and strategies. Telephone conferencing is especially useful to interview experts from other countries.)

9. Account executives, analysts, and portfolio managers at brokerage firms receive information and commentaries from many internal and external publishers. Ask them to cycle these materials to investment committee trustees.

Anyone can be an expert. It just takes reading. Improved investment returns and greater personal satisfaction are the rewards.[7]

NOTES

1. This paraphrases a story attributed to Bernard Baruch.
2. The Penn Central commercial paper crisis.
3. No one I know who has provided information ever felt the journalist got it 100 percent right.
4. Nathan E. Davis, *Being Right or Making Money,* (Nokomis, Fla.: Ned Davis Research, Inc., 1991), p. 40.
5. This is the author's memory of a presentation by a Dean Witter analyst who discovered more than 30 profitable stocks in less than 10 years.
6. Peter Lynch, *One Up on Wall Street,* (New York: Simon & Schuster, 1989), pp. 181–82.
7. A human resource counselor argues that anyone can be an expert by reading in one field two hours per day. See Appendix 4 for my favorite books and periodicals.

CHAPTER 17

A MEETING OF THE "COLLEGE" INVESTMENT COMMITTEE*

An idea cried out; it said, "Let me in: I can improve the world by improving relationships!"

The plane takes off. Twenty minutes pass. John Reimer and Doris Dock relax. They think. A meal is served.

"What happened today?" asks Doris.

"I don't know," says John, "but it might be the most fruitful investment committee meeting I've ever attended. It was informal, but by the end we were getting things done, and professor Buehler's presentation about his recent trip to the European Community was fascinating. Why did they invite him?"

"I don't know, really, but it gave me a sense that the college is exciting. If I were back in school, I'd immediately register for one of his courses, and it even made me feel that our work is worthwhile, that the returns we are attempting to achieve are used for something constructive in real life. I wish our retirement plan accounts would do the same thing—you know, invite in a department head or an engineer to tell us about the company's products or a personnel officer to let us know how employees feel about their retirement plan accounts."

"The student they invited to attend scared me to death," says John.

"Me too," responds Doris. "I feared that everything we said might be in the student newspaper. She appeared out of place and at first very nervous, but when she got to talking about her opinion of the board of trustees, I both laughed and cried, because I've seen so many of the types she described, the superserious overseers of money, minds, and methods."

"During a break," John adds, "President Topp told me that she is a straight-A student majoring in economics and that she probably will

*This is fictional.

step up to run her family's business in a few years. I think he is trying to give her an early experience in college governance because he thinks she will be a business leader and a potentially large contributor 5 or 10 years from now. Apparently, the board elects one recent graduate every year as a trustee, and they use meetings like ours to evaluate which students are strong candidates for that board position."

Doris then says, "Probably. Anyway, regardless of the college's motives, she made a revealing observation about student attitudes when we were discussing social investing and potential restrictions on new investments. She said, I think, that students are moving toward encouragement of investing in South Africa. They think it is time to be more involved, to help the people there. What a change from 20 years ago! It was students, you know, who started the social investing movement; if we had paid attention to them then, we would have avoided all those expensive liquidation transactions. Anyway, she suggested that some students might be more interested in investing than we think. Didn't she mention a young man who has done well in the national stock selection contest?"

"Yes. I've heard about that contest, and it appears to be more a game of luck than of skill because it runs only nine months, but this one young man apparently spent the summer reading about investment opportunities in Chile. He then spent time with a student from Chile whose father runs a large dairy, and before he was done he even talked to the father by telephone. Anyway, the result was that he purchased Chilean stocks and almost won the national contest."

"Maybe we should talk to him."

"Let's. I wouldn't mind having a few bright kids on the waiting list to work for us."

"How come we made decisions so quickly today?" asks Doris.

"Yeh. That was intriguing. It was like they all knew what they were talking about. The one fellow, George, I think, gave an incredible report about collateralized mortgage obligations, and I thought for a moment he was going to recommend purchase of CMOs with every available dollar from every single endowment and scholarship fund, until Bill put it on the line. What did he say? Something like, 'George, calm down. It's a great investment area, but you sound like a man who just found water on the desert. Why don't you buy one personally and see how it goes? Meanwhile we can discuss it with the consultant to see how it fits our policy.' "

"Very direct, don't you think!" comments Doris.

"Yes, but George took it well. Looks like they all get along."

"I guess they have worked together a couple of years, not long enough to be great friends, but apparently members of this investment committee meet informally for dinner whenever they can, like one-on-one when one visits the town of another. That itself is an idea. Maybe we should suggest it to all our clients. If members of our client committees just knew each other better, the meetings would be more comfortable and probably more productive."

"I don't know," John replies. "We'd have to be careful how we suggest it, because most of our accounts don't appear to want to hear personal advice."

"True, but this meeting was so effective. It was amazing! I didn't know they had sent the controller to that asset allocation conference in Chicago last month. His report was a little sloppy because he misused words now and then, but the effect was positive. Right after, Sharyl remembered that a group in her town, possibly the local Society of Financial Analysts, was planning local educational programs that she could attend."

"This committee will know more than we do," John says. "It could be tough on us if they decide to do it all themselves."

"Sure, but that's unlikely," Doris replies. "They would need full-time staff and support equipment that would cost more than our fee, and I felt that they respect what we are trying to do. After lunch, Ted, the committee chairman, told me that he really appreciates our extra effort in coming over on a Saturday, and he personally hopes that we can do business together for many years. Incidentally, he also asked me how often I think we should meet."

"What did you say?"

"I was in a good mood, so I said never."

"Did he laugh?"

"A little. He was not resentful. He said, 'These sessions probably don't improve our rate of return, but they sure make us feel better, and we learn just a little bit more about ourselves, the college, and the economy. We need to see you now and then, if only because we like you.' "

"Great response," John says. "Knowing him, he probably meant it. The chairperson before him was a real piece of work. Thought he knew everything, and he did know a lot, but I always felt that he would know twice as much if he just stopped moving his lips a minute or two."

"I remember him," Doris recalls. "I don't know what happened, but the rumor was that the committee bounced him. Evidently, Sharyl just told him to his face that she felt left out and intimidated because he dominated every conversation and did not distribute data. Then he said that he honestly was tired of the responsibility and wanted to quit. So he quit."

John then observes, "And today's meeting was so smooth. Everyone seemed comfortable, even Professor Buehler and, by the end, the student. It was interesting how Ted started informally, allowing everyone to chat and to express a few opinions, but then he became more formal. Toward the end, he was using parliamentary procedure to keep people on track, to prevent them from chatting about issues not under consideration.

"Yes, it was a very well-run meeting. I sensed that Ted had called every committee member personally, in advance, to see if they wanted to make any specific points. There was no sense that motions and results were predetermined, but nothing surprised the chair."

"Could be," Doris says. "An old friend of mine who served several terms as a state legislator told me about his personal cardinal rule: 'Never surprise the chair.' I believe he felt that advising the chair in advance greases the wheels."

"I enjoy meeting dynamics," says John, "but the best part for me was when the new trustee, Phil White, started asking about vague language in their investment policy."

"Do you think we can work with him?" Doris asks.

"Good point. I guess he was appointed our contact person. He's supposed to interpret both our results and our commentaries. Since he's new, it won't be easy at first, but it might turn out to be easier than working with someone who already thinks he knows everything. Maybe we should invite him to New York. I'd sure like to, but there's that old bugaboo that the college might not have enough money to send him, and it is unethical for us to pay for it. I wish we could resolve that dilemma!"

"Speaking of dilemmas," says Doris, "I wonder if we ever can work things out with the consultant community. Those folks alternately drive me crazy, then surprise me with strokes of brilliance. For years, my opinion has been that their only goal is to conduct manager searches—in other words, to replace us or to prevent us from getting more capital from our current clients. But then I say to myself they're OK because they keep more useful data than anyone else and they do relieve us from the teaching responsibility, especially during policy-writing time. But then something else happens, like the time Dave of Consult, Ltd., forced me into a long and irrelevant public discussion about why our purchase of a stock, probably Chrymac, fit well due to its negative correlation with everything else. That group never did understand covariance, and some days I'm not sure I understand it myself.''

''You know, though,'' says John, ''I was talking to a West Coast consultant a few months ago. Apparently they, too, have problems with client perceptions. He said that boards want to do manager searches; it gives them something to do, a reason to meet. Also, he seldom is satisfied with policies he himself helps draft because they go through so many reviews and compromises that by the end they read like undercooked French toast. Then I asked if he helps people and he said, 'Yes, I do. I frequently help clients avoid problems with ERISA, and I'm sure that our client/boards take more risks than they would if we were not involved. Also, every once in a while, we effectively dissuade a board from making a wasteful new manager search. In these cases, our numbers prove that it is statistically impossible to diversify further. Manager searches are very expensive, particularly if you add the value of volunteer time,' Then I asked him to tell me the most common reason boards and committees make poor decisions. He answered, 'Fatigue.' I myself have wondered about the influence of fatigue, because committees frequently subject themselves to long days of interview after interview after interview. At the end, everyone is so tired they just want to make a quick decision and get home to take off their shoes.''

''How do you think the college will handle proceeds from the new capital campaign?'' Doris asks. ''Do you think they and the consultant will set up the type of multiday parade of potential managers that we luckily survived five years ago? Even I was tired that day, just from sitting outside the committee room four hours while others did their song and dance. What a waste of time. I could have been back in the office doing something useful. But we got the account, though I have no idea how.''

''No question, that was a tough day,'' John says, ''but I bet they'll do it differently next time. They were well organized today, and I thought I heard Ted talking about it with the consultant. But I sure know how I wish they would do it. I wish they would let each of their current managers—especially us—make a case for allocating new funds to present managers. We all could do this in writing, and the investment committee trustees could make a preliminary decision from written proposals because they already know us so well. This would be inexpensive. On the other hand, if they need to do a new manager search, I wish they would go see prospective managers in person."

"I don't know," responds Doris. "They might need to search in new areas. For one, they don't have an international manager, and now they are big enough to hire a full-time cash manager."

"True," John replies. "They would have to search if they allocate to new asset classes, but I still wish they would travel to see the managers. In part, my sense of cost is talking. If they interview eight managers, all appearing in person, sometimes with two representatives, think of the total hotel and travel expenses! I bet if we did not budget new client presentations, we could reduce fees."

"Maybe. But that's unrealistic; our boards can't or won't do it. I wonder if telephone or video conferencing would be effective? There ought to be a better way."

"Still," says John, "it was a great day. This committee has it together. They were attentive and respectful, and I respect them. I couldn't believe they decided to publish their investment policy and results. Every financial organization in the country now will call trying to get in the door, but I'll wager they pick up good ideas from the calls. Our business changes so fast that it's hard to keep up, and good new ideas appear in unexpected places. Anyway, it was a good day. Incidentally, to change the subject, what did you think of that magazine column suggesting that beta is dead as a useful risk measure? I think he might be right. On the other hand. . . ."

APPENDIX 1

HYPOTHETICAL AGENDA: MEETING TO CREATE AN INVESTMENT POLICY

1. Opening statement by the chair.
2. Self-introductions:
   a. Name and so forth.
   b. Personal experiences.
   c. Comments about the organization; recent actions of participants' other committees.
   d. New perceptions about investing from recent experiences or reading.
3. Review of organization's vision and strategic goals.
4. Consideration of characteristics of a cogent investment policy:
   a. Understandable to a "competent stranger" or "reasonable man."
   b. Specific and measurable.
   c. Written.
   d. Reproduced in the minutes of the board.
   e. Records debate, including all points of view.
   f. Subject to periodic review at planned intervals.
5. Risk assumption, with projection of corresponding return:[1]
   a. How to measure risk?
   b. How much risk can we *afford?*
   c. How much risk can we *tolerate?*
   d. Written statement of acceptable risk.
   e. Time period over which risk is accepted.
   f. Return expected from assuming risk.
6. Permissible assets.
   a. Are there any unacceptable asset classes? Why? Write down reasons.
   b. Are any specific companies or types of companies unacceptable by policy or custom? List and explain in writing.
   c. Review again unacceptable assets. Be sure written language is precise and does not *unintentionally* exclude some investment opportunities. Ask consultant to comment on intelligibility of language.

    d. Discuss risk and return of each asset class.

    e. List permissible asset classes.

    f. Allocate fund among asset classes.

    g. Reconsider risk of the *entire* portfolio.

7. Performance:

    a. How important is performance? (Some committee members believe that performance is extremely significant, while others focus on philosophy instead.)

    b. What is the interval for measurement?

    c. To meet organization's real objectives (to pay retirement benefits, serve the community, etc.), must total return exceed a standard (often called a benchmark or, more informally, a bogey)?

    d. What are acceptable results?

8. Professional services:

    a. Bank or brokerage custodian.

    b. An auditor.

    c. Independent performance measurement.

    d. Data about funds of similar organizations.

    e. Periodic economic and market information.

    f. Professional investment managers.

        (1) How many?

        (2) What type?

9. Engaging professional services:

    a. Is a competitive bid required?

    b. Referrals.

    c. Interviews.

    d. Formal search through a consultant.

10. Creation of monitoring system:

    a. Content and frequency of reports, and method of distribution.

    b. Frequency of committee meetings.

    c. Reports to the board.

11. Spending policy:

    a. Empowerment to spend.

    b. Realized returns compared to total returns. (Realized returns are interest, dividends, and appreciation realized through sales of securities; total return includes unrealized appreciation.)

    c. Board's cash flow expectation. (Does the board expect more income from the account than the investment committee believes is sensible?)

12. Reexamination of decisions:

    a. Have important views been spurned or ignored?

b. Is any participant uncomfortable? Who? Why?

c. Should decisions be unanimous?

13. Following a *break,* reading and approval of documents.

14. Adjournment.

Ideas for Better Meetings

1. Prior to the meeting, each committee member shall have read at least one book regarding portfolio theory, investment policy, or the relationship between investment and spending.

2. The chair must assure that each committee member may speak without restriction.

3. Due to the economics of travel and hotels, multiday meetings might have to be held on successive days. But, if feasible, it is better to have rest days between meeting days.

4. The breakfast gathering should be relaxed and unstructured. Lunch and dinner might include short talks by investment experts or reviews of recent literature by committee members.

5. Meetings managed by professional facilitators often produce superior results.

6. There should be plenty of time for rapport building and relaxation.

7. A secretary or consultant must keep detailed records of the meeting. Copying equipment should be available.

8. Organizations creating policy may use a professional consultant to help design the meeting and to interpret results. However, they should avoid interviewing professional money managers prior to setting policy. When interviews occur first, there is a tendency to write policy that accommodates the committee's favorite candidates.

NOTE

1. "Ends management theory" would suggest stating goals first, as in "We want to earn 15 percent per year for five years," then calculating the risk required to achieve the goal. However, most committees initially set a high goal only to find themselves having unacceptable risk. Then they push down the goal until everyone is comfortable with the risk. On the other hand, by first spending more time on risk, committees will find that they can accept more risk than originally deemed possible, and this will tend to push the reward goal higher.

APPENDIX 2

HYPOTHETICAL AGENDA: ROUTINE REVIEW MEETING

1. Opening statement by the chair.
2. Self-introductions and personal comments.
3. Consultant's presentation.
4. Managers' presentations
   a. Results.
   b. Reasons for results.
   c. Strategy for coming period.
   d. Report of any changes in manager's organization.
5. Comparison of results and strategies to the established investment policy.
6. Amendments to policy (proposed amendments circulated before the meeting).
7. Presentation by committee to managers and consultants about recent developments in the organization. (It is best to do this first when the committee is hearing reports from many different managers and consultants. This procedure allows the professionals to return to work following their presentations.)
8. Questions.
9. Approval of report to the board.
10. Adjournment.

Additional Ideas for Effective Meetings

1. There is a complete exchange of documents *in advance;* every participant sees every document; managers receive consultant's report; consultant receives managers' reports.
2. Each money manager delivers oral report in executive session to avoid inadvertent exchange of proprietary concepts and direct confrontation among competing opinions.
3. Committee members may receive written economic forecasts and market predictions from brokers, money managers, or the consultant. Therefore, these are not part of the meeting agenda.

4. The seating arrangement should be cooperative, not adversarial. This is not a congressional hearing. Everyone is coequal and shares the same goal of increasing the assets of the organization.

5. Committee members concerned about specific transactions, results, or strategies should discuss these concerns with the managers and consultants *before* the meeting. A meeting should not be tied up in discussing a few transactions. Changes in strategy should be discussed only in the context of a proposal to amend the investment policy.

6. It is just as important for money managers and consultants to understand the purposes of the organization as it is for committee members to understand financial results and strategies. Therefore, the meeting includes a discussion of recent events in the organization.

7. There must be a complete written record, including points of dissension.

8. Suggested frequency of meetings: once a year, half-day. (If more than a half-day is required, consider having two meetings per year to keep each meeting short.)

APPENDIX 3

INVESTMENT COMMITTEE TRUSTEES

JOB DESCRIPTION OF AN INVESTMENT COMMITTEE TRUSTEE

Each member of the investment committee is expected to perform the following duties:

1. Prepare himself or herself for this responsibility by:
   a. Attending seminars.
   b. Reading investment literature, especially on modern portfolio theory, manager and consultant selection, investment policy, performance measurement, asset allocation, and the psychology of investing.
   c. Reading professional investment periodicals such as the *Financial Analysts Journal*, mutual fund reviews, and publications about nonprofit and retirement plan management.
2. Assist in preparation of investment and spending policies.
3. Assist in hiring professional consultants and managers.
4. Assure that risk actually assumed by money managers is equal to risk prescribed in the investment policy.
5. Monitor investment performance.
6. Determine if potential future investment returns are sufficient to support the goals of the institution. If not, suggest either that potential returns should be increased by assuming more risk or that goals should be more realistic.

CHARACTERISTICS OF INVESTMENT COMMITTEE TRUSTEES

Rare is the board that matches jobs and talents. Nevertheless, there is considerable agreement about qualifications of successful investors. They include:

1. Patience: ability to evaluate events calmly in the context of long-term trends and institutional goals.
2. Courage: personal convictions and willingness to make decisions.

3. Intelligence: usually just common sense.
4. Emotional stability: capacity to distinguish fact from emotion.
5. Hard work: willingness to give time.
6. Predisposition to understand and to embrace risk.
7. Curiosity.
8. Flexibility: openness to new ideas.
9. Committee competence: intuitive understanding of how boards/committees achieve; in large committees, committee competence includes knowledge of rules of order.[1]

QUESTIONNAIRE FOR PROSPECTIVE INVESTMENT COMMITTEE MEMBERS

The purpose of this questionnaire is to locate individuals *motivated* to deal with investment policy; it is not to identify experience. Therefore, a selection committee should look for enthusiasm in the responses. An individual who demonstrates enthusiasm by providing thoughtful answers will work harder than one who merely lists experiences.

Questionnaire

The board of directors is seeking individuals to serve on the investment committee. If you are interested, please respond to these questions either in writing or by calling a current investment committee member. We do not expect detailed, technical answers.

1. Why do you want to serve on the investment committee?
2. Describe your experiences investing personal funds.
3. Have you assisted in investment policy creation for institutions such as retirement plans or endowments? What was your function and contribution? Were results satisfactory?
4. What do you think are the important responsibilities of an investment committee member?
5. What methods would you employ to improve investment results?
6. What methods would you propose to improve the efficiency and effectiveness of the investment committee?
7. If you have no investment experience, how do you propose to learn to invest?
8. What is the relationship between investment policies and the success of our institution?
9. What business periodicals do you read, or propose to read?

NOTE

1. Some ideas drawn from Douglas H. Bellemore, "Characteristics for Success as Aggressive Investors," quoted in *Classics,* ed. Charles Ellis (Homewood, Ill.: Business One Irwin), 1989, p. 309.

APPENDIX 4

PERSONAL READING EXPERIENCES

My reading home runs occurred during games I was forced to attend. The first was a required economics course. I had to read *The Crash of 1929,* by John Kenneth Galbraith. It is a captivating study of the late 1920s, and an important history. It also was my first lesson about the power of myths and the importance of original research. I had assumed that thousands of people had jumped from buildings as their personal net worths declined, but Galbraith looked up facts. Using New York City records, he found that suicides remained constant during most of the 20s and 30s. A revelation: Popular beliefs are not always true!

Another big score occurred during my Dean Witter training in 1969. I was asked to read Gerald Loeb's *The Battle for Investment Survival,* a collection of newspaper columns. It was readable and enjoyable! It used common language to describe common sense! Up until then, I thought business literature was lifeless and boring. Loeb proved it can be fun, practical, and entertaining. Peter Lynch's *One Up on Wall Street,* as well as the essays and speeches of Sir John Templeton, similarly make plain the deceivingly simple task of searching for good investments.

As part of a continuing education course by the College for Financial Planning, I read two more home runs. The first was Charles Ellis's absorbing *Investment Policy: How to Win the Loser's Game.* It should be required for every stock broker, investment advisor, amateur investor, and trustee. In 78 pages, it defines challenges and obstacles, and nudges readers to have reasonable expectations.

The college also required me to study *Selected Readings in Investment Strategies and Portfolio Management,* compiled by the college staff in 1987. The readings are instructional. They explain concepts and techniques, as well as beta, economic and market cycles, psychology, investment models, diversification, and many other topics.

Classics: An Investor's Anthology and *Classics II: Another Investor's Anthology,* both edited by Charles Ellis, reprint excerpts from the best of investment literature. Each 15- to 20-minute chapter stands alone. They are enlightening, and some are entertaining. For financial health, take one each night before lights out.

I've enjoyed books about Wall Street debacles and intrigues. They provide momentary pleasure, but none has stimulated insight into playing the investment game. On the other hand, John Train's book *Famous Financial Fiascos* is both amusing and useful; it might help its readers avoid confidence games.

Mr. Train also has been a columnist for *Forbes* and is the author of two superb books about money managers: *The Money Masters* and *The New Money Masters*. Both were resources for this book. He probably had two goals: (1) to identify and describe the personal human characteristics of great investors, and (2) to use those skills to improve his own management of portfolios. While reading these two books, I've wondered if investment committees should change their selection process. In place of asking managers about their techniques, personnel, and past performance, look instead for personality characteristics described by Train. Another idea is to create national investment competitions similar to violin and piano competitions.

A Brief History of Time from the Big Bang to Black Holes, by physicist Stephen W. Hawking, has influenced my attitudes about investing. He describes the uncertainty principle and quantum mechanics with this relevant declaration: "One certainly cannot predict future events exactly if one cannot even measure the present state of the universe precisely!"[1] The problem is that the measurement device affects the object measured, a hypothesis that also describes investors' relationships to markets.

The scientific approach to markets is well represented by *The Founders of Modern Finance: Their Prize-winning Concepts and 1990 Nobel Lectures,* published by the Association of Investment Management and Research, which contains the foundations of modern portfolio theory and the 1990 Nobel laureate lectures.

I encountered another home run through the board of the International Association for Financial Planning. Executive director Janet Crane asked me and other board members to hear audiotapes by John Carver. The tapes prompted me to read his book *Boards That Make a Difference.* As a result, I now believe investment committees should devote 25 percent of meeting time to evaluating their effectiveness.

Related works on effectiveness are *Robert's Rules of Order* and the newer *Sturgis Standard Code of Parliamentary Procedure.* Embodied in these ingenious instructions is a philosophy of productiveness and respect for group dynamics. The rules require boards to consider one thing at a time and to hear everyone's relevant opinions. If someone pontificates about subjects not on the table, he or she may be declared "out of order" so that the board can proceed to a conclusion. Persons who study Robert's or Sturgis become effective themselves by learning how to approach a group, to make motions, and to obtain seconds; they learn the difference between expressing opinions and getting things done.

While examining my business, I found that the government can help. The Federal Reserve, for example, publishes extensively, and the *Federal Reserve Bulletin* contains enough economic data for anyone's appetite. Information about demographics is available through state agencies that study census data. In my state, an agency forwards a newsletter at no charge.

The demands of business, continuing education, and volunteer service have directed my reading, and affiliations with trade and educational institutions have provided the opportunities. These groups are the International Association for Financial Planning (IAFP), the Institute of Certified Financial Planners (ICFP), the Association for Investment Management and Research (AIMR), the Indiana University Center on Philanthropy, and the Council on Foundations. They offer books, magazines, conferences, and audiotapes. Especially useful are AIMR pamphlets on asset allocation and performance presentations. Meanwhile, the *Financial Analysts Journal,* the *Chronicle of Philanthropy, Pensions and Investments,* the *Journal of Financial Planning* and *Foundation News,* have been very important to me. I also subscribe to the *Harvard Business Review.* It has thoughtful articles (and outstanding cartoons). Trustees should look for additional publishing programs in their alma maters and in educational and "think tanks" in their hometowns.

Trustees interested in the raw data of finance should keep in touch with the work of Ibbotson Associates (securities markets as a whole), Morningstar (mutual funds), and Performance Analytics (private money managers), as well as data provided by numerous consultants, associations, and trade organizations.

GUIDE TO PERIODICALS

This list includes scholarly periodicals available to trustees at reasonable cost. Newspapers have been excluded. An asterisk (*) indicates a highly recommended periodical. Readers who have time should consult *Ulrich's International Periodicals Directory,* the Business and Economics—Investments section, for additional suggestions.

AAII Journal
American Association of Individual Investors
625 N. Michigan Avenue
Chicago, Illinois, 60611
Helps individual investors become more effective managers of their own assets.

American Stock Exchange Annual Report
American Stock Exchange Inc.
86 Trinity Place
New York, New York 10006-1881

The Chronicle of Philanthropy
Chronicle of Higher Education, Inc.
1255 Twenty-Third Street, N.W., Suite 700
Washington, D.C. 20037-1125
Occasional article or book review about investing.

Dick Davis Digest
P.O. Box 9547
Fort Lauderdale, Florida 33310-9547
Investment philosophies, analysis, and stock market recommendations.

Federal Reserve Bulletin
U.S. Federal Reserve System
Board of Governors of the Federal Reserve System
Publications Services, Room MS-138
Washington, D.C. 20551
Economic statistics; minutes of meetings.

Financial Analysts Journal[*]
Association for Investment Management and Research
Box 3668
Charlottesville, Virginia 22903
Portfolio management studies; commentaries; drafting policies; book reviews; legal and regulatory issues.

Financial Management
Financial Management Association
University of South Florida, College of Business
Tampa, Florida 33620-5500
Research papers; two journals; annual investment conferences.

Forbes
60 Fifth Avenue
New York, New York 10011
Frequent data on mutual funds, investment strategies, and market performance.

Foundation News
Council on Foundations
1828 L. Street, N.W.
Washington, D.C. 20036
Occasional articles on investments; sponsors investment seminars for members.

Global Money Management
Institutional Investor, Inc.
488 Madison Avenue
New York, New York, 10022
International investment management.

Harvard Business Review*
Harvard University
Graduate School of Business Administration
Soldiers Field Road
Boston, Massachusetts 02163
Case studies; business ethics; business management; social issues.

Hulbert Financial Digest
316 Commerce Street
Alexandria, Virginia 22314
Rates performance of financial newsletters and reviews investment strategies.

Institutional Investor*
Institutional Investor, Inc.
488 Madison Avenue
New York, New York 10022
Portfolio management, investment banking, book reviews, ranking of analysts.

Investment Companies
CDA/Wiesenberger Investment Companies Services
CDA Investment Technologies
1355 Piccard Drive
Rockville, Maryland 20805

Journal of Business
University of Chicago Press
Journals Division
P.O. Box 37005
Chicago, Illinois 60637

Journal of Financial Planning
Institute of Certified Financial Planners
7600 E. Eastman Avenue, Suite 301
Denver, Colorado 80231
Primarily individual financial planning, with occasional articles about mutual funds, ERISA, and investment strategies.

Journal of Futures Markets
John Wiley & Sons, Inc., Journals
605 Third Avenue
New York, New York 10158-0012

Journal of Portfolio Management*
Institutional Investor, Inc.
488 Madison Avenue
New York, New York 10022
Theoretical concepts.

Managed Accounts Reports Inc.
220 Fifth Avenue, 19th Floor
New York, New York 10001
Managed futures.

Nasdaq Fact Book & Company Directory
National Association of Securities Dealers, Inc.
1735 K St., N.W.
Washington, D.C. 20006-1506
Extensive data on the performance of the Nasdaq stock market and the securities
trading in it; includes names, addresses, and phone numbers of each company
listed in the Nasdaq national market and the Nasdaq small-cap market.

Pensions & Investments*
Crain Communications, Inc.
220 East 42nd
New York, New York 10017-5806
Broad coverage of practical and legal issues; numerous directories and statistics;
sponsors conferences.

Pension World
Communication Channels, Inc.
6151 Powers Ferry Road NW
Atlanta, Georgia 30339

Stocks, Bonds, Bills and Inflation Yearbook*
Ibbotson Associations, Inc.
225 N. Michigan Avenue, Suite 700
Chicago, Illinois 60601-7676
Extensive tables on returns, risk and inflation; most theoreticians start with this
data; commentaries on recent year; sponsors excellent conferences on asset allocation.

SPECIFIC ARTICLES

Curran, John J. "Why Investors Make the Wrong Choices." *Fortune, 1987 Investor's Guide,* p. 63 ff.

O'Hanlon, John, and Charles Ward. "How to Lose at Winning Strategies." *Journal of Portfolio Management,* Spring 1986, p. 20.

Shefrin, Hersh and Meir Statman. "The Disposition to Sell Winners Too Early and Ride Losers Too Long: Theory and Evidence." *Journal of Finance,* July 1985, p. 777.

Tognazzini, Donn V. "Steps to Successful Fund Management for Small, Medium Sized Firms." *Pension World,* October 1992.

Tverksy, Amos, and Daniel Kahneman. "The Framing of Decisions and the Psychology of Choice." *Science,* January 30, 1981, p. 453.

NOTE

1. Stephen W. Hawking, *A Brief History of Time,* (Toronto, Canada: Bantam Books, 1988), p. 55.

GLOSSARY

accrual   Investors frequently own benefits not yet paid. If a bond pays interest in January and July, by the end of March an owner is entitled to three months' interest. The owner of a stock is entitled to the dividend after the ex-dividend date, though it may not be paid for several weeks. These are accruals, and they should be included in any computation of total value on a specific date.

actuarial calculations   Statistical predictions about the future costs of employee benefit plans. The actuary assumes life expectancies and a rate of return on invested capital, predicts the amount and timing of liabilities (benefits), and tells the company how much additional capital it must contribute each year to meet those liabilities.

AIMR   Association of Investment Management and Research (formerly Financial Analysts Federation); the association of investment professionals; dedicated to investment research; confers the prestigious CFA (chartered financial analyst) designation.

allocation, allocator   See *style*.

alpha coefficient   The difference between the actual performance of a fund and the performance it should have achieved on a risk-adjusted basis. What a fund "should have achieved" depends on several assumptions. Theoriticians use this statistic to present the value added by a money manager.

arbitrage   Simultaneous purchase and sale of the same or related securities in different markets in order to make a profit as unequal prices become equal; occasionally involves securities of companies to be acquired or merged; an investment management style that seeks arbitrage profits.

asset   A single investment or specific security; usually a stock or bond; any item on the left side of a balance sheet.

asset allocation   The investment committee process of dividing portfolios between cash, debt, and equity, or a money management style in which the manager changes the percentages of assets in these and other categories according to his or her economic or market forecasts.

balanced   Used to describe a fund with allocations to several asset classes, commonly stocks, bonds, and cash.

beta coefficient   A statistic that measures the volatility (risk) of an asset against the volatility of the market in which it is traded; a stock having a beta of 1.1 has been approximately 10 percent more volatile than the stock market as a whole; *low beta* and *high beta* sometimes are used incorrectly to mean "conservative" or "speculative."

bottom-up   See *style*.

cash   Once meant hard currency, such as physical dollars and coins. Now refers to money left in checking or short-term savings accounts, in money market funds, or in "cash equivalents," which are securities that have short maturities; cash is an earning asset.

common trust fund   Like a mutual fund, but administered by a bank for its trust customers, including employee benefit plans.

conservative   1. A cautious, low-risk investor.   2. An asset or portfolio likely to change moderately in value with few, if any, major unexpected (downward!) adjustments; opposite of *speculative;* an investor or portfolio biased toward fixed income; although used often in a comparison ("We are more conservative than _____"), it is impossible to quantify with precision, but statistics like beta, variance, and standard deviation are used to apply objective standards to subjective terms like *conservative* and *aggressive*.

contrarian   Used to describe someone who believes, "I think differently than everyone else," the dilemma being that most contrarians are self-proclaimed. (Everyone wants to be a successful contrarian since it implies that everyone else is wrong.) Contrarians buy securities that nobody else wants (at the moment!). See also *style*.

core   Of course, the central part of anything; therefore, "core holdings" acquired by a "core manager" form the central assets of a portfolio that are held passively for long periods. Frequently refers to securities of large companies, or "blue chips;" unfortunately, no two investors agree on a specific list of core securities.

consultant   A company or individual who provides educational information, analyzes results, and provides assistance and guidance for such tasks as money manager searches. In this book, the word occasionally is used to mean any person who gets things done: the facilitator or motivator of action such as the staff member or trustee who coordinates meetings, contacts professionals, and keep records.

correlation coefficient   A very useful statistical concept for analyzing portfolio risk, it measures the strength of covariance. A positive 1.0 means that two assets rise and fall in the same direction at the same time at the same rate; a negative 1.0 means that one asset has declined by the same magnitude that another has risen; zero means no relationship at all between two assets. If a portfolio manager wants to reduce risk defined as volatility, he or she needs to purchase diverse assets that are negatively correlated (i.e., that are known to move in opposite directions), thereby smoothing the total result.

coupon Originally, the detachable portion of a bond certificate redeemable for cash on a specified date; now used interchangeably with *interest*, as in, "The bond has an 8 percent coupon," meaning it pays interest of 8 percent per year ($80 per $1,000 face amount).

covariance A measurement of whether two variants in a time series have tended to move in the same direction (a positive absolute number) or in the opposite direction (a negative number). If Stock A and Stock B have both tended to rise and fall together at the same time, their covariance is positive. See *correlation coefficient*.

custodian Financial institution that holds securities, usually a bank or brokerage firm. If broad services are provided, a custodian might be known as a "master trustee."

debt securities Bonds.

defined benefit and defined contribution Two types of employee benefit plans. In the former, employees know (through a formula) what they will receive. In the latter, the sponsor pledges an annual contribution amount while benefits vary in part with investment returns.

default A failure; a bond that does not pay principal and/or interest when due.

directed brokerage Circumstance in which a board of trustees or other fiduciary requests its money manager to direct commissions to a particular broker in exchange for specific services; see *soft dollars*.

dollar-weighted See *time-weighted*.

Dow Jones Industrial Average A price-weighted, largely passive average of 30 large, well-known industrial stocks that tend to be leaders of their industry and are listed on the New York Stock Exchange. It is the most famous, most widely quoted measurement of the market, and is often incorrectly interpreted as a general measure of economic activity and securities price movements. It has been adjusted over the years for stock splits and other changes.

duration "The average time required for the investor to recover [the discounted present value of] his investment and the interest on it"[1] by combining the effect of the maturity and the size of coupon payments. Some managers and/or sponsors explain their risk policies and/or styles by duration.

earnings   Profit after all expenses and taxes, usually expressed per share.

efficient frontier   Part of modern portfolio theory. A portfolio having the greatest possible return at a given level of risk is "efficient." The widely reproduced graph of all possible efficient portfolios is the "frontier." The point is that an investor theoretically can select an "ideal" portfolio by first determining either the level of acceptable risk or the desired potential return, then knowing immediately the other parameter.

employee stock ownership plan (ESOP)   A retirement-oriented savings program in the employer's own stock; usually the plan borrows to purchase the stock.

equity   Used to mean ownership; especially of common stocks.

fiduciary   Any person or entity having responsibility for someone else's money.

fixed income   1. As in "I live on a fixed income," means "I live on stated retirement benefits that probably will not increase" or "My income is not too high."   2. As in *fixed-income security* means a bond or preferred stock whose payments will not change.   3. As in *fixed-income portfolio,* means a group of fixed-income securities. Caution: the total return and principle value of a fixed-income portfolio is anything but fixed due to continuous changes in current market value; also, recently introduced variable-rate bonds and preferreds now are included in the meaning of *fixed-income portfolio.*

fundamental   Facts (such as elements in a company's accounting statements) and analysis of facts considered basic and direct, such as actual value of a company's property and annual earnings, amount of debt compared to equity, and products produced; see *technical.*

futures   Originally, contracts to purchase and sell agricultural commodities and industrial materials at specified prices on future dates; contracts now available on financial instruments. "Managed futures" is an asset class available to plan sponsors.

growth   1. A company whose earnings improve every year (implies above-average rate of annual improvement).   2. A stock or portfolio that has appreciated and is likely to continue doing so.   3. See *style.*

hard dollars   Specified fees payable in cash directly against an invoice; see *soft dollars.*

hedge   A transaction or strategy designed to reduce risk; usually also reduces potential reward.

high-yield   A class of bonds having high interest payments and therefore high risk. These bonds are rated lower quality (less than Baa) by credit evaluation services. See *junk*.

income   Cash payments such as salary, dividends, or interest. However, *income-oriented* is an ineffectual, seldom-quantified term apparently used to declare, "We want cash now."

index, index fund   A named measurement of a market's time-weighted performance such as the Standard & Poor's Index of 500 stocks or the Lehman Long-Term Bond Index. Some mutual funds and investment managers attempt to duplicate index performance by purchasing all assets that compose the index.

intermediate   The middle of a time frame, usually one to five years for fixed-income securities; see *short*.

issuers   Legal term found in national and state securities laws; commonly means a company or governmental entity that sponsors securities sold to the public.

junk   An ill-starred term applied in the early 1980s to high-yield bonds. Though widely used, it is not specific and is unprofessional due to its connotation of "throwaway."

laddered portfolio   A portfolio of bonds with approximately equal par amounts coming due in successive years.

large cap stocks   Modern version of category once known as "blue chip"; older, seasoned companies, having total capital in excess of $2 billion or thereabouts; see *small cap*.

Lehman Brothers bond indices   The aggregate bond index, the government/corporate bond index, the government bond index, and others; market value-weighted measurements against which many managers and investors measure performance. Other investment banking firms such as Solomon Brothers also sponsor indices.

load   The commission on a mutual fund or partnership.

long   1. see *short*.   2. As in "long the stock," the condition of owning a security as reflected on the accounts of a custodian.

long-term   Used but seldom quantified in investment policies; difficult to define because it often is used as a sweeping generality, as in "I am a long-term investor" or "The investment goal of our organization is long-term"); for fixed income securities, implies maturities longer than 10 years.

manager   As in "money manager," individual or firm that selects specific investments for the portfolio.

managed futures   The management of futures that originally were contracts to purchase and sell agricultural commodities at future dates but recently include stock and bond indexes, currencies, and precious metals.

margin   A no-no for most trustees; implies borrowing to purchase securities, thus increasing risk beyond widely accepted prudence; more precisely, the down payment an investor must make before borrowing takes place; for example, at 50 percent required margin rates, an investor must deposit $500 of his money to purchase $1,000 worth of securities.

market cycle   As in ''our goal is to exceed the rate of return of the S&P 500 Index over one market cycle.'' By hindsight, the distance from peak to peak or trough to trough in the economy, a class of securities, or the stock market as a whole; impossible to quantify looking forward. (In the stock market, a cycle usually is measured from bear market low to the next bear market low, which tends to occur every four years.)

master trust   Multifunction pooling of assets to handle custody, apportionment of funds among different money managers, and accounting.

modern portfolio theory (MPT)   See Chapter 11, pages 93–97.

moving average   An average measured over successive time periods. The average closing price of a stock over the last 200 days is a moving average if it is recalculated every day for the trailing 200 days. A moving average is used by market technicians to describe trends and by timers to predict trends.

mutual fund   Professionally managed investment company that commingles funds from many investors to create a diversified portfolio of securities. Individuals occasionally buy and sell mutual funds like stocks, assuming that they are a specific capital asset. Mutual funds are managed like large private accounts.

options   Contracts to buy (call options) or sell (put options) securities at a specific price before a specific date; used both to hedge and to speculate.

plan sponsor   Parent organization of a benefit plan such as an employer or nonprofit.

price-earnings ratio (PE ratio)   A fraction in which the numerator is share price, the denominator recent or projected net profit per share; one of the oldest and most fundamental statistics for measuring value.

profit-sharing plan   Retirement plan that receives contributions as a percentage of the sponsoring company's profits.

prudent man   A concept born of an 1829 Massachusetts court decision that said, ''All that can be required of a trustee to invest, is, that he shall conduct himself faithfully and exercise a sound discretion. He is to observe how men of prudence, discretion and intelligence manage their own affairs, not in regard to speculation, but in regard to the permanent disposition of their funds, considering the probable income, as well as the probable safety of the capital to be invested.''

qualified plan   Retirement plan that meets legal requirements for a tax deduction of contributions and tax deferral on plan earnings. Pension and profit sharing plans, as well as 401(k)s and individual retirement accounts (IRAs), are qualified plans.

range   The distance between the high and low prices of a security for a specified period; used to consider either value ("It is at the low end of its range") or risk ("It trades over a wide range").

relative strength   Measurements relative to a standard; routinely computed for stocks, industries, and indexes; considered a resource to predict trends. If a stock is selling today above its 200-day average price, it has a positive strength relative to its average.

risk   Probability of a negative occurrence such as a decline in market value. Unlike specific probability percentages for life expectancy, risk of a heart attack, or risk of an automobile accident, investment risk has been defined as volatility around an average, apparently to demonstrate that actual returns might be different from expected returns. Beta, standard deviation, mean absolute duration, and range are used to quantify financial risk.

risk-free rate of return   The return on 90-day Treasury bills. However, finance needs a better term because nothing is free of risk; nevertheless, certain economic models require a "risk-free" point of departure.

screening   The initial step in selecting specific securities for inclusion in a portfolio; results in a list of acceptable alternatives; commonly implies sorting for desired characteristics by computer.

securities   Intangible instruments that have value, such as stocks, bonds, certificates of deposit, mutual funds, options, warrants, and futures contracts.

short   1. As in *short maturity*, varies by investment category. (A cash manager believes "short" is only several days while "long" is 60 to 90 days; a bond manager believes "short" is 1 to 5 years while "long" is up to 30 years). 2. A brokerage account is "short" if it has not yet received securities recently sold.   3. As in *to short the stock*, a method of borrowing and selling to make profits on declining securities.

small cap stocks   Usually, stocks issued by newer companies (occasionally called emerging growth companies) that have accumulated less than $500 million in total capital. Historically, small capitalization stocks have produced greater returns but higher volatility than large cap stocks, because it is easier to grow when you are small.

soft dollars   Commissions paid to brokers by money managers in exchange for services such as research, governed under Section 28(e) of the Securities and Exchange Act of 1934. Usually, the broker calculates the real, or "hard-dollar," price of the services, then offers to accept commissions instead at three to five times the hard-dollar amount. See *directed brokerage.*

speculative   Refers to a transaction, stock, or portfolio that has greater-than-average potential reward commensurate with greater-than-average risk; implies the goal of quick profit; opposite of *conservative;* not a "bet" or a "gamble" that depends on a single chance occurrence, but the risk of a venture. Of course, one person's "speculation" is another person's core holding.

standard deviation   The dispersion of outcomes around a mean; a good measure of risk because it reflects probability. Approximately two thirds of all observations occur within one standard deviation. The mean is an average of many values, such as stock prices, investment returns, trading volume, and so on, but it does not give an impression of the total range of those values. If the standard deviation is 10 percent, then two thirds of the values used to compute the mean occur within 10 percent of that mean; in other words, the greater the standard deviation, the greater the volatility or risk.

Standard & Poor's 500 Index   The composite of 500 stocks (the S&P 500) widely used as a benchmark to which individual account performance is compared. Mutual funds and common trust funds have been organized to duplicate this index. Standard & Poor's indexes also include several other market indexes and over 90 industry indexes.

styles   The perceived techniques that allow categorization of money managers; difficult intellectual concept due to wide disparities within the categories. Different statistical services define categories differently. Some styles are:

- **allocators**   Those who divide the total fund between equities and cash according to their prediction of which asset class will do well.
- **balanced managers**   Those who mix all types of stocks and bonds to achieve a balance and to have involvement with potential industry or sector moves wherever and whenever they occur; seldom consider any form of market timing.
- **bottom-up managers**   Those who start the analytical process at the bottom of the economy by first looking at consumer trends and other basic economic preferences, finding companies that benefit by those preferences, then determining if those companies fit portfolio strategy.

- **contrarians** Those who find value where no one else is looking by purchasing securities from unpopular or unconventional asset classes or industries.
- **core managers** Those who purchase securities at the "core" of the economy—basic, important industries.
- **growth (or earnings growth) managers** Those who seek securities of companies predicted to return profits rising at a greater annual rate than average; includes *emerging growth managers,* who look for newer companies, and *quality growth managers,* who have a qualitative measurement such as size, name recognition, stability, and ability to pay dividends.
- **index managers** 1. Equity managers who purchase securities by computer to match the composition and weightings of an index. 2. Bond managers who attempt to match the performance of an index by purchasing securities similar to those in the index.
- **market-oriented** 1. Those who purchase securities that typically act like the market as a whole. 2. Those whose styles cannot be more precisely defined.
- **price-driven managers** Those to whom the price of a security is the most important criterion; similar to *value-driven managers.*
- **rotators** Those who move funds between market sectors or industries attempting to be at the right place at the right time.
- **screeners** Those who rely heavily on computers. Selection starts with a computer screen that lists all securities that meet the manager's statistical criteria; a typical screen might look for all stocks having earnings growth of at least 15 percent per year, a price-earnings ratio of 20 or less, and a dividend yield of 3 percent or more. Most managers consider their screens proprietary and confidential.
- **timers** Those who attempt to buy low and sell high by application of a timing theory. "Buy when price-earnings ratios are less than 10, and sell when they are more than 15" is a timing theory. Timing theories start with a hypothesis that is tested against historical data to see if it would have been successful had it been applied in the past.
- **top-down managers** Those who approach analysis and selection from the top (i.e., national policy and the economy) to find companies that will benefit by current macroeconomic trends.
- **value managers** Those who select securities based on today's relative value (instead of trends). *Value* either is a perception or computation that a security is inexpensive compared either to a standard or to other, similar

securities. If Retailer X sells at 10 times earnings while Retailer Y sells at 20 times earnings, Retailer X has value.

- **yield managers**   Those who seek securities that have high dividend or interest income.

systematic risk   Risk inherent to an entire environment or system; see *unsystematic risk*.

technical   Used to describe an approach involving facts and analysis of facts that indirectly reflect basic value; includes numerous phenomena such as relative strength, moving averages, exchange volume figures, and patterns on price charts; see *fundamental*.

time-weighted and dollar-weighted   Two methods of computing a total rate of return on a portfolio. Their very existence is a message to investors: *Be sure two sets of data are comparable*. The time-weighted method counts each period equally, ignoring cash flows such as new contributions and expenditures; the dollar-weighted method, often called internal rate of return method, includes net cash flows, thereby providing a better measure of a manager's contribution. Unfortunately, other methods also exist to confuse trustees.

total return   Both realized and unrealized gains as well as income. The term is widely misunderstood and sometimes bitterly debated. Total return is often a published investment objective, usually a compromise between those trustees who advocate "growth" and those who advocate "income." It is the standard for performance comparisons between funds because it includes both income and growth as the investment manager's entire contribution to a plan sponsor.

trends   Calculated, charted, and graphed ratios, yields, prices, averages, and other data useful to analysts.

trustee   1. As used in this book, an individual responsible for someone else's money.   2. A company or an individual who performs fiduciary duties prescribed in a trust document.

unsystematic risk   A risk pertaining to one element in a large environment or system. The risk of one stock is unsystematic, while the risk of the entire market of which it is an element is systematic.

warrant   A contract that gives the owner the right to purchase a security at a specific price through a specific date.

Wilshire 5000 Equity Index   One of the most inclusive indexes; based on the dollar value of all New York Stock Exchange and American Stock Exchange listed securities, plus the most active issues in the over-the-counter market.

wrap fee Contractual arrangement with financial institutions such as brokers in which one fee covers all services (investment management, custody, performance measurement, and commissions on transactions).

yield Usually, a stated rate of cash return such as the coupon rate of a bond or percentage dividend rate of a stock.

NOTE

1. Arthur Williams III, *Managing Your Investment Manager,* (Homewood, Ill. 1986), Business One Irwin, p. 277.

BIBLIOGRAPHY

BOOKS ON INVESTING

Ellis, Charles D. *Classics.* Homewood, Ill.: Business One–Irwin, 1989.

———. *Classics II.* Homewood, Ill.: Business One Irwin, 1991.

———. *Investment Policy: How to Win the Loser's Game.* Homewood, Ill.: Business One Irwin, 1985.

Gibson, Roger C. *Asset Allocation.* Homewood, Ill.: Business One Irwin, 1990.

Hirt, Geoffrey A. and Stanley B. Block. *Fundamentals of Investment Management,* 2nd ed. Homewood, Ill.: Business One Irwin, 1986.

Ibbotson Associates, Inc. *Stocks, Bonds, Bills, and Inflation.* Yearly.

Institute of Chatered Financial Analysts. *Managing Investment Portfolios: A Dynamic Process,* 2nd ed. Boston: Warren, Gorham & Lamont, 1990.

Massy, William F. *Endowments: Perspectives, Policies & Management.* Association of Governing Boards of Universities and Colleges: Washington D.C., 1990.

Train, John. *The Money Masters,* New York: Harper & Row, 1980.

———. *The New Money Masters,* New York: Harper & Row, 1989.

Throne, Don; Bill Albright; and Bill Madden. *Procedural Prudence: The Fiduciary's Handbook for Management of Retirement Plan Assets.* SEI Wealth Management Services, 1991.

Williams, Arthur. *Managing Your Investment Manager.* Homewood, Ill.: Business One Irwin, 1992.

BOOKS ON GOVERNANCE

Carver, John. *Boards That Make a Difference.* San Francisco: Jossey-Bass, 1991.

Conrad, William R., and William E. Glenn. *The Effective Voluntary Board of Directors.* Athens, Ohio: Swallow Press, 1976.

Hall, Peter Dobkin. *Inventing the Nonprofit Sector.* Baltimore: The Johns Hopkins University Press, 1992.

Houle, Cyril O. *Governing Boards*. San Francisco: Jossey-Bass, 1989.

O'Barr, William M., and John M. Conley. *Fortune and Folly: The Wealth and Power of Institutional Investing*. Homewood, Ill.: Business One Irwin, 1992.

Shandler, Michael. *Planning Inspired Performance Program*. Atlanta, Ga.: The Atlanta Consulting Group, Inc., 1988.

MISCELLANEOUS BOOKS

Perret, Gene, and Linda Perret. *Funny Business*. Englewood Cliffs, N.J.: Prentice-Hall, 1990.

Thoughts on the Business of Life. New York: Forbes, Inc., 1968.

INDEX